FOUNDATIONS

Steven J. Molinsky

Bill Bliss

PRENTICE HALL REGENTS

A VIACOM COMPANY

Upper Saddle River, NJ 07458

Publisher: *Tina Carver*
Director of Production: *Aliza Greenblatt*
Editorial Production/Design Manager: *Dominick Mosco*
Page Layout/Composition: *Siren Design*
Manufacturing Manager: *Ray Keating*

Art Director: *Merle Krumper*
Interior and Cover Design: *Bill Smith Studio*
Photographer: *Paul Tañedo*
Illustrator: *Richard Hill*
Art Production/Scanning: *Todd D. Ware, Marita Froimson, Don Kilcoyne*

PRENTICE HALL REGENTS
A VIACOM COMPANY

© 1996 by PRENTICE HALL REGENTS
Prentice-Hall, Inc.
A Division of Simon & Schuster
Upper Saddle River, New Jersey 07458

10 9 8 7 6 5 4 3 2 1

ISBN 0-13-384604-0

Prentice-Hall International (UK) Limited, *London*
Prentice-Hall of Australia Pty. Limited, *Sydney*
Prentice-Hall Canada Inc., *Toronto*
Prentice-Hall Hispanoamericana, S.A., *Mexico*
Prentice-Hall of India Private Limited, *New Delhi*
Prentice-Hall of Japan, Inc., Tokyo
Simon & Schuster Asia Pte. Ltd., *Singapore*
Editora Prentice-Hall do Brasil, Ltda., *Rio de Janeiro*

Contents

8   Food • Supermarkets • Restaurants   93

9   Colors • Clothing • Shopping   107

10   Money • Banking   119

TO THE TEACHER

Foundations is an all-skills textbook that offers low-beginning level students of English the basic vocabulary and language they need to communicate in essential lifeskill situations — Personal Information; Everyday Activities; The Classroom; Housing and Furniture; Numbers, Time, and Calendar; The Community; Describing People and Things; Food, Supermarkets, and Restaurants; Colors, Clothing, and Shopping; Money and Banking; Health and Medicine; The Post Office, School, and Library; Occupations and Work Skills; Directions and Transportation; and Weather and Recreation.

The text builds language and vocabulary *foundations* through a variety of dynamic, interactive exercises and activities that develop students' basic listening, speaking, reading, and writing skills.

Foundations is designed as the pre-beginning text for *Side by Side, ExpressWays, Classmates,* or any other beginning-level textbook. For additional vocabulary enrichment, *Foundations* is correlated with the *Word by Word Basic Picture Dictionary.*

An Overview

Chapter-Opening Illustrations

Each chapter of *Foundations* begins with an illustration that depicts the key vocabulary and language presented in the chapter. Students can describe the illustration and make predictions about what the people might be saying to each other. In this way, students have the opportunity to share the vocabulary words they already know and relate the chapter theme to their own lives and experiences.

Guided Conversations

Guided conversations are the dialogs and exercises that are the essential learning devices in *Foundations*. Model conversations depict situations in which people use the key vocabulary of each lesson. In the exercises that follow, pairs of students create their own conversations by placing new vocabulary items into the framework of the model. A "skeletal dialog" that appears after the model provides students with a helpful framework for doing the exercises.

Follow-Up Exercises and Activities

A variety of follow-up exercises and activities reinforce and build upon the vocabulary items and essential language presented in the guided conversation lessons.

- **Language in Motion** activities get students moving around the classroom as they ask each other questions and gather information.

- **Games** motivate active learning through small-group and full-class practice.

- **Writing** activities offer basic practice with authentic lifeskill writing tasks.

- **Listening** exercises develop students' aural comprehension skills.

- **Construction Site** exercises offer practice with key grammatical structures. (Grammar is not emphasized in *Foundations,* but is highlighted when important structures are needed for communication practice.)

- **Community Connections** activities help students become aware of resources available in the community.

- **Information Gap** activities get students working in pairs as they compare information to complete a task.

- **Different Cultures, Different Ways** sections highlight cross-cultural differences.

- **Language Experience Journal** writing activities promote early student writing on topics of high interest and relevance.

Support and Reference Sections

End-of-chapter Summaries include the following:

- **Vocabulary Foundations** — a listing of the key vocabulary in the chapter for review.

- **Language Skill Foundations** — a self-assessment listing of important lifeskills presented in the chapter.

Listening Scripts are provided for all listening exercises in the text.

A *Foundations/Word by Word Basic* **Correlation** provides a listing of the units in *Word by Word Basic* that offer additional vocabulary enrichment for each *Foundations* chapter.

Suggested Teaching Strategies

We encourage you, in using *Foundations*, to develop approaches and strategies that are compatible with your own teaching style and the needs and abilities of your students. While the text does not require any specific method or technique in order to be used effectively, you may find it helpful to review and try out some of the following suggestions.

Chapter-Opening Illustrations

Activate students' prior knowledge of the vocabulary of each chapter by having students look at the illustrations and tell the words they already know. Write the words on the board and have students practice reading and saying them. Also, have students predict what the people might be saying to each other. Students in pairs or small groups may enjoy practicing the conversations and then presenting them to the class.

Guided Conversations

1. **SETTING THE SCENE:** Have students look at the model photograph in the book. Set the scene: Who are the people? What is the situation?

2. **LISTENING:** With books closed, have students listen to the model conversation — presented by you, by a pair of students, or on the audiotape. Check students' understanding of the situation and the vocabulary.

3. **CLASS PRACTICE:** With books still closed, model each line and have the whole class practice in unison.

4. **READING:** With books open, have students follow along as two students present the model.

5. **PAIR PRACTICE:** In pairs, have students practice the model conversation.

6. **VOCABULARY PRESENTATION:** Present the new vocabulary words in the exercises. Point to the photograph of each item, say the word, and have the class repeat it chorally and individually. Check students' understanding and pronunciation of the vocabulary.

7. **THE SKELETAL DIALOG:** Write the "skeletal dialog" on the board. Fill in the replacement from Exercise 1 to show students how the guided conversation method works. Call on a few pairs of students to practice Exercise 1 using the skeletal framework on the board.

8. **EXERCISE PRACTICE:** (optional) Have pairs of students simultaneously practice all the exercises.

9. **EXERCISE PRESENTATIONS:** Call on pairs of students to present the exercises.

Community Connections

Have students do the activity individually, in pairs, or in small groups and then report back to the class.

Different Cultures, Different Ways

Have students first work in pairs or small groups, reacting to the photographs and responding to the questions. Then have students share with the class what they talked about.

Put It Together!

In these paired *information gap* activities, Student A has information that Student B doesn't have, and vice versa. The object is for students to ask each other questions in order to fill in the missing information.

Language Experience Journal

An important component of *Foundations'* mission is to show students how writing can become a vehicle for communicating thoughts and feelings. Have students begin a Language Experience Journal in a composition notebook. In these Language Experience Journals, students have the opportunity to write about things that are meaningful to them.

Depending on your students' writing abilities, either have them write in their journals or dictate their story for you to write. Then you or your students should read what they have written to a classmate. If time permits, you may also want to write a response in each student's journal, sharing your own opinions and experiences as well as reacting to what the student has written. If you are keeping portfolios of students' work, these journal entries serve as excellent examples of students' progress in learning to write in English.

In conclusion, we have attempted to offer students of English at the low-beginning level a communicative, meaningful, and lively way of learning the basic vocabulary and language they need to communicate in essential lifeskill situations. Through listening, speaking, reading, writing, discussion, movement, games and other activities, our goal has been to take advantage of students' different learning styles and particular abilities and strengths.

While conveying to use the substance of our textbook, we hope that we have also conveyed the spirit: that learning basic language, vocabulary, and lifeskill needs can be genuinely interactive . . . relevant to our students' lives . . . responsive to students' differing strengths and learning styles . . . and fun!

Steven J. Molinsky
Bill Bliss

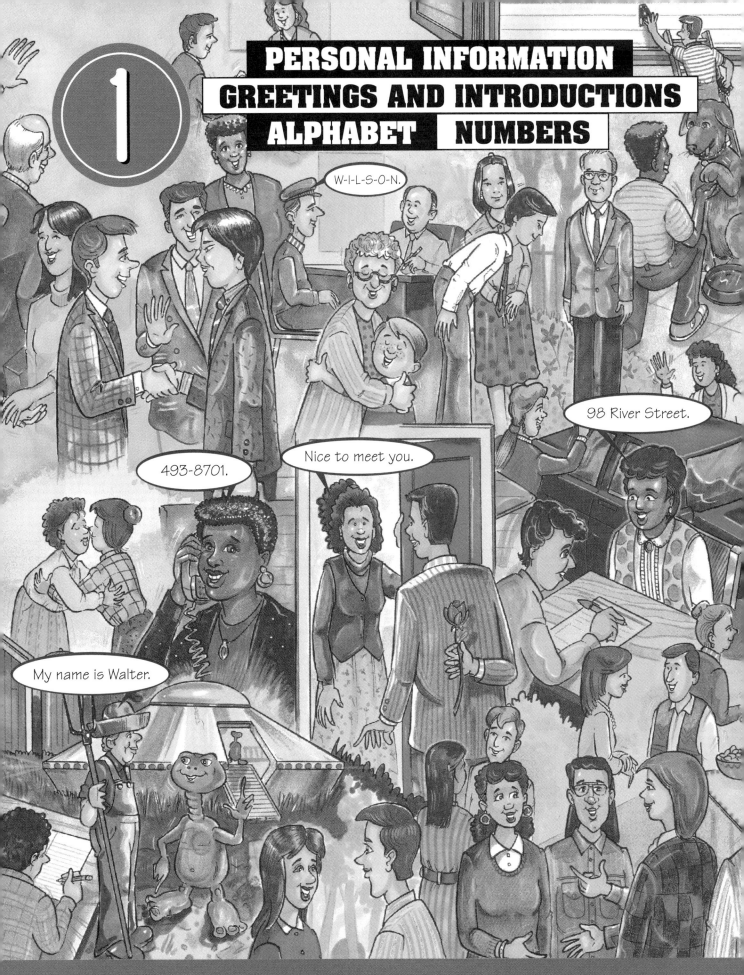

INTRODUCE YOURSELF

A. Hello. My name is Trung Dong.

B. Hi. I'm Carmen Fernandez. Nice to meet you.

A. Nice to meet you, too.

Practice conversations with a partner. Use your first and last names.

A. Hello. My name is _____ _____.

B. Hi. I'm _____ _____.
Nice to meet you.

A. Nice to meet you, too.

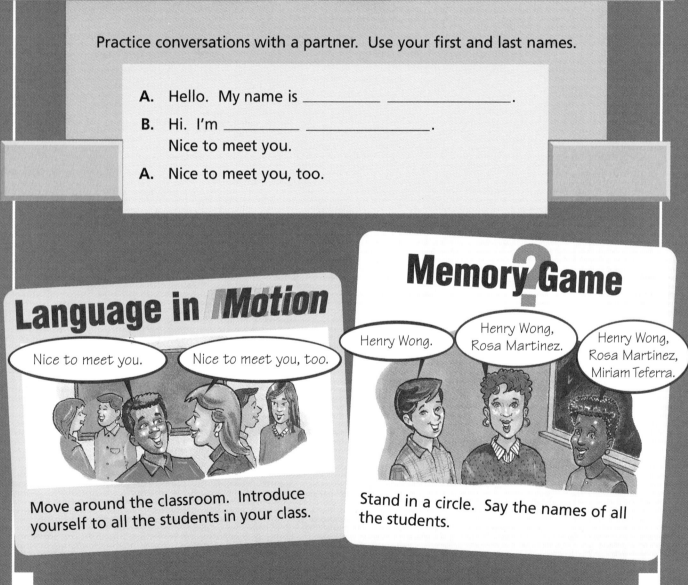

Language in Motion

Nice to meet you.

Nice to meet you, too.

Move around the classroom. Introduce yourself to all the students in your class.

Memory Game

Henry Wong.

Henry Wong, Rosa Martinez.

Henry Wong, Rosa Martinez, Miriam Teferra.

Stand in a circle. Say the names of all the students.

Circle the letters in your first name.

(A) B (C) D E F G H I J (K) (L) M N (O) P Q (R) (S) T U V W X Y Z

Write your first name.

CARLOS

FIRST NAME

C	A	R	L	O	S						

First Name

C	A	R	L	O	S						

First Name

Circle the letters in your first name.

A B C D E F G H I J K L M N O P Q R S T U V W X Y Z

Write your first name.

_____

FIRST NAME

First Name

First Name

Circle the letters in your last name.

A B C D E F G H I J K L M N O P Q R S T U V W X Y Z

Write your last name.

_____

LAST NAME

Last Name

Last Name

SPELL YOUR NAME

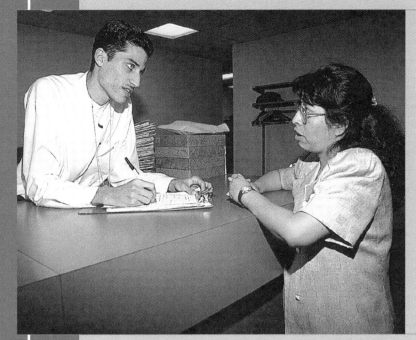

A. What's your last name?

B. Ramirez.

A. How do you spell it?

B. R-A-M-I-R-E-Z.

Practice conversations with a partner. Spell your last names.

A. What's your last name?

B. _____.

A. How do you spell it?

B. _____.

Listening

Listen and circle.

1. (K-E-L-T-O-N)   C-L-A-Y-T-O-N

2. B-R-E-N-N-E-R   K-R-A-M-E-R

3. K-W-A-N   P-H-A-N

4. S-A-N-D-E-R-S   S-A-N-C-H-E-Z

5. D-R-A-K-E   B-L-A-C-K

6. L-E-E-S   G-R-E-E-N

Missing Letters

Write the missing letters.

A B C D <u>E</u> F G H I J K L <u>M</u> N O P Q R S T U V W X Y Z

What word do the letters spell? <u>N</u> <u>A</u> <u>M</u> <u>E</u>

Write the missing letters.

__ B C D E F G H I J K __ M N O P Q R __ __ U V W X Y Z

What word do the letters spell? ___ ___ ___ ___

Write the missing letters.

A B C D E __ G H __ J K L M N O P Q __ __ __ U V W X Y Z

What word do the letters spell? ___ ___ ___ ___ ___

Language in Motion

Move around the classroom. Make a list. Write the first and last names of all the students in your class.

What's your first name?
How do you spell it?
What's your last name?
How do you spell it?

Give Your Telephone Number

0	zero
1	one
2	two
3	three
4	four
5	five
6	six
7	seven
8	eight
9	nine
10	ten

A. **What's your telephone number?**

B. **293-1807.**

A. **Is that 293-1807?**

B. **Yes.   That's correct.**

Practice conversations with a partner. Use your phone numbers or make up phone numbers.

A. What's your telephone number?

B. _____.

A. Is that _____?

B. Yes. That's correct.

Language in Motion

973-2437.

Move around the classroom. Ask all the students for their phone numbers. Use real phone numbers, or make up phone numbers.

Digital Display Numbers

1	2	3	4	5	6	7	8	9	10

Missing Numbers

Write the missing numbers.

1   2   *3*   4   ___   6   7   8   ___   10

1   ___   3   ___   5   ___   ___   8   9   ___

Listening

Listen and circle.

1. (463-9221)   463-9112
2. 984-1673   948-6137
3. 249-1115   245-1119
4. 728-3030   728-0303
5. 671-2098   671-2058
6. 837-1234   837-1284

Matching

Match the words and numbers.

1. three   7
2. ten   1
3. seven   3
4. two   6
5. six   10
6. one   2

COMMUNITY CONNECTIONS

Write these important telephone numbers.

 Police: _____

 Ambulance: _____

 Fire: _____

POISON

Poison Control Center: _____

Give Your Address

11	eleven
12	twelve
13	thirteen
14	fourteen
15	fifteen
16	sixteen
17	seventeen
18	eighteen
19	nineteen
20	twenty
21	twenty-one
22	twenty-two
30	thirty
40	forty
50	fifty
60	sixty
70	seventy
80	eighty
90	ninety
100	one hundred

A. **What's your address?**

B. **15 Center Street.**

A. **Did you say 50 Center Street?**

B. **No. 15 Center Street.**

Practice conversations with a partner. Use your address, or make up addresses.

A. What's your address?

B. _____.

A. Did you say _____?

B. No. _____.

Language in Motion

10 Main Street.

Move around the classroom. Ask all the students for their addresses. Use real addresses, or make up addresses.

Pronunciation

Practice these pairs of numbers.

13 - 30

14 - 40

15 - 50

16 - 60

17 - 70

18 - 80

19 - 90

Listening

Circle the number you hear.

1. 55   (59)
2. 16   60
3. 30   13
4. 70   77
5. 12   20
6. 19   90
7. 34   44

Form Information

What's the name of your city? _____

What's the name of your state? _____

What's the abbreviation of your state? ☐ ☐

What's your zip code? _____

Some Abbreviations

California	CA
Florida	FL
Illinois	IL
New York	NY
Texas	TX

Fill Out the Form

NAME ⊢┬┬┬┬┬┬┬┬┬┬┬┬┬┤ ⊢┬┬┬┬┬┬┬┬┬┬┬┬┬┬┤
FIRST   LAST

ADDRESS ⊢┬┬┬┬┬┬┬┬┬┬┬┬┬┬┬┤
NUMBER   STREET

⊢┬┬┬┬┬┬┬┬┬┬┤ ⊢┬┤ ⊢┬┬┬┬┤
CITY   STATE   ZIP CODE

TELEPHONE ⊢┬┬┤ ⊢┬┬┬┬┬┤
AREA CODE   NUMBER

INTRODUCE FAMILY MEMBERS

A. **This is my husband.**

B. **Nice to meet you.**

C. **Nice to meet you, too.**

A. **This is my wife.**

B. **Nice to meet you.**

C. **Nice to meet you, too.**

Practice conversations in groups of three. Introduce family members.

A. This is my _____.

B. Nice to meet you.

C. Nice to meet you, too.

1. mother

2. father

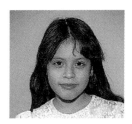

3. daughter

4. son

5. sister

6. brother

7. grandmother

8. grandfather

Where Are Your Family Members?

What family members live in your home?

_____

What other family members live in this country?

_____

What family members live in other countries?
Where do they live?

_____

_____

More Family Vocabulary
- aunt
- uncle
- niece
- nephew
- cousin
- granddaughter
- grandson

Language in Motion

Bring in photos of your family members. Move around the classroom. Ask and answer questions about your family members.

A. Who is this?

B. This is my daughter.

A. What's her name?

B. Her name is Angela.

A. How old is she?

B. She's 3 years old.

A. Who is this?

B. This is my grandfather.

A. What's his name?

B. His name is Gustavo.

A. How old is he?

B. He's 78 years old.

A. Who is this?

B. This is my ——————.

A. What's her/his name?

B. Her/His name is ——————.

A. How old is she/he?

B. She's/He's ——————.

A FAMILY TREE

Anna

Victor

Linda

Daniel

Paul

Carla

Finish the sentences about this family tree.

1. Anna is Victor's _____wife_____.
2. Linda is Anna and Victor's _____.
3. Linda is Paul and Carla's _____.
4. Carla is Anna and Victor's _____.
5. _____ is Linda and Daniel's son.
6. _____ is Paul and Carla's father.
7. _____ is Paul and Carla's grandmother.
8. _____ is Linda's husband.

Now work with a partner. Make more sentences about this family tree.
How many sentences can you make?

_____   _____
_____   _____
_____   _____

Language Experience Journal

My Family Tree

Begin a Language Experience Journal in a
composition notebook. Your journal is a place for
your own writing. In your journal, draw your family
tree and write a story about your family. Or, tell
the story so your teacher can write it. Then read
your story to a classmate.

DIFFERENT CULTURES | DIFFERENT WAYS

People greet each other in different ways in different cultures.

Some people
shake hands.

Some people hug.

Some people kiss.

Some people
bow.

In your culture, how do people greet friends?
How do people greet each other at work?
How do children greet their parents?

PUT IT TOGETHER PART A

Work with a partner. One person looks
at this page. The other person looks at
page 14. Ask each other questions and
fill out the job application form.

What's the person's
first name?

Cathy. What's her
last name?

Kwan.

```
Name            _____Kwan_____
                First         Last

Address    1244_____
                Number    Street

           Long Beach                90815
                City       State   Zip Code

Telephone _____

Social Security Number  062-83-4796_____
```

INFORMATION
GAP
ACTIVITY

Work with a partner. One person looks at this page. The other person looks at page 13. Ask each other questions and fill out the job application form.

What's the person's first name?

Kwan.

Cathy. What's her last name?

Name   Cathy
         First   Last
Address   Edison Street
         Number   Street
                         CA
         City   State   Zip Code
Telephone (310) 472-9813

Social Security Number _____

Vocabulary Foundations

Hello	mother
Hi	father
	daughter
name	son
first name	sister
last name	brother
telephone number	grandmother
address	grandfather
city	aunt
state	uncle
zip code	niece
social security number	nephew
spell	cousin
	granddaughter
wife	grandson
husband	

Language Skill Foundations

I can . . .

☐ introduce myself

☐ spell my name aloud

☐ give my telephone number

☐ identify important emergency telephone numbers

☐ give my address

☐ introduce family members

☐ check my understanding

☐ give correction

☐ print the letters of the alphabet

☐ write numbers

☐ fill out a simple form with personal information

☐ draw and describe my family tree

☐ compare greetings in different cultures

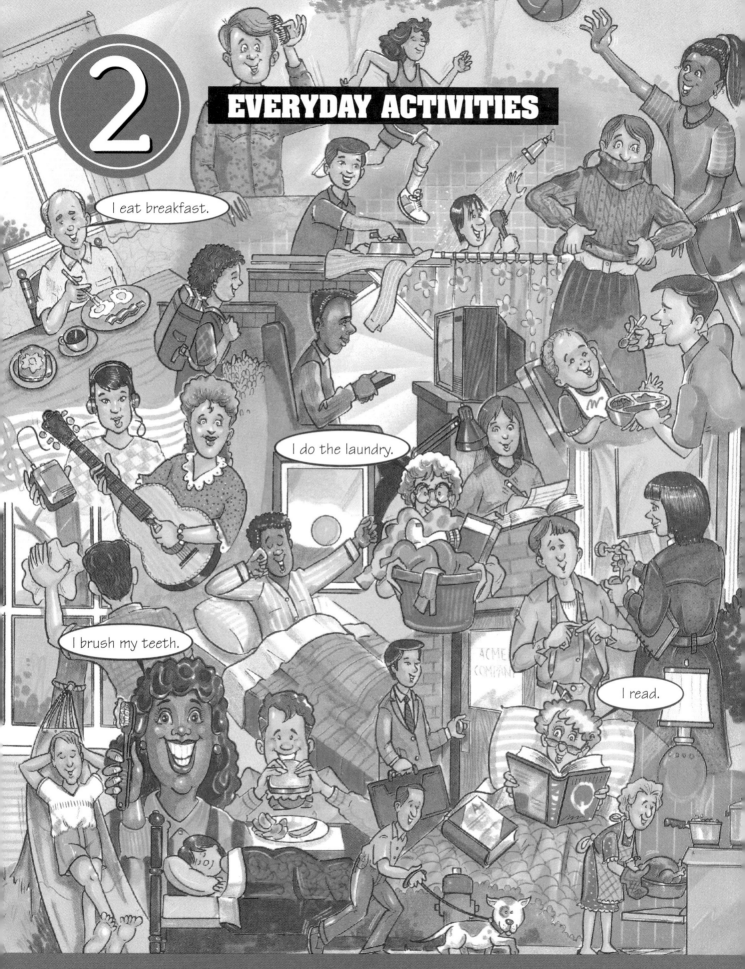

2 EVERYDAY ACTIVITIES

These people are telling things they do every day. What are they saying?

I get up.

I take a shower.

I brush my teeth.

I comb my hair.

I get dressed.

I eat breakfast.

I go to work.

I go to school.

I eat lunch.

I come home.

I cook dinner.

I read.

I watch TV.

I get undressed.

I go to bed.

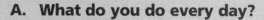

A. **What do you do every day?**

B. **I get up, I get dressed, I eat breakfast, and I read.**

Practice conversations with a partner. Use everyday activities.

A. What do you do every day?

B. I _____, I _____, I _____, and I _____ .

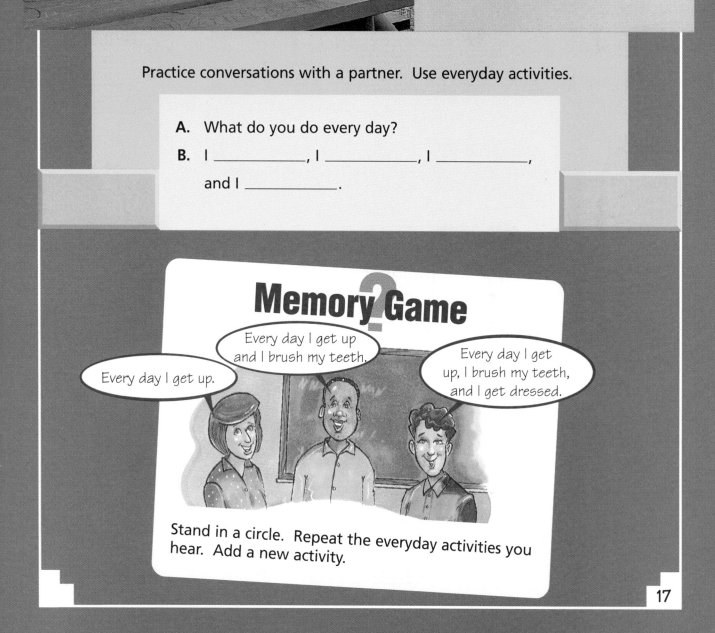

Memory Game

Every day I get up.

Every day I get up and I brush my teeth.

Every day I get up, I brush my teeth, and I get dressed.

Stand in a circle. Repeat the everyday activities you hear. Add a new activity.

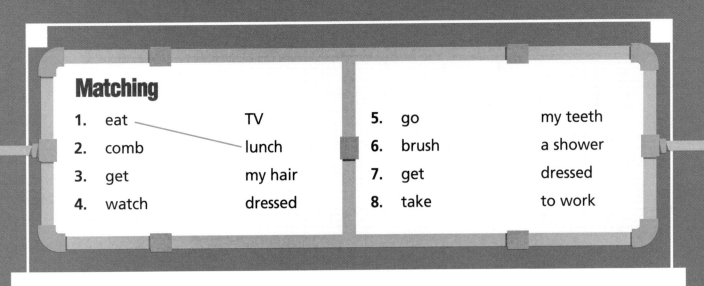

Matching

1. eat — — — — lunch
2. comb
3. get   my hair
4. watch   dressed

5. go   my teeth
6. brush   a shower
7. get   dressed
8. take   to work

Listening

Listen and put a check under the activity you hear.

1. ✓ _____   _____
2. _____   _____

3.   _____   _____
4. _____   _____

5.   _____   _____
6. _____   _____

7.   _____   _____
8. _____   _____

18

What's the Order?

Put these actions in the correct order.

1. __2__ I take a shower.
   __3__ I go to work.
   __1__ I get up.

2. ____ I go to bed.
   ____ I go to school.
   ____ I get dressed.

3. ____ I come home.
   ____ I go to work.
   ____ I eat breakfast.

4. ____ I eat lunch.
   ____ I get up.
   ____ I comb my hair.

5. ____ I eat dinner.
   ____ I eat breakfast.
   ____ I eat lunch.

6. ____ I go to bed.
   ____ I get undressed.
   ____ I get up.

COMMUNITY CONNECTIONS

Write the information.

My School

The Place Where I Work

Name _____ _____

Address _____ _____

_____ _____

Phone Number _____ _____

Right Now at Home

I'm making breakfast.

I'm making lunch.

I'm making dinner.

I'm cleaning.

I'm washing the dishes.

I'm doing the laundry.

I'm ironing.

I'm feeding the baby.

I'm walking the dog.

I'm studying.

I'm exercising.

I'm listening to music.

I'm playing the guitar.

I'm playing basketball.

I'm relaxing.

WHAT ARE YOU DOING?

A. Hi! What are you doing?

B. I'm cleaning. How about you?

A. I'm making breakfast.

Practice conversations with a partner. Use everyday activities.

A. Hi! What are you doing?

B. I'm _____. How about you?

A. I'm _____.

Language in Motion

Pantomime an everyday activity. Other students guess the activity.

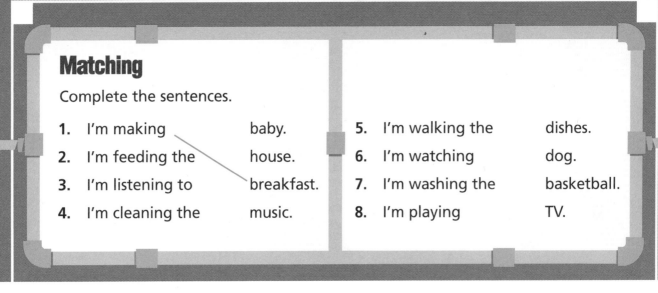

Matching

Complete the sentences.

1. I'm making   baby.
2. I'm feeding the   house.
3. I'm listening to   breakfast.
4. I'm cleaning the   music.

5. I'm walking the   dishes.
6. I'm watching   dog.
7. I'm washing the   basketball.
8. I'm playing   TV.

Listening

Listen and put a check under the activity you hear.

1. ✓

2.

3.

4.

5.

6.

7.

8.

Construction Site

Every day **I read.**

Right now **I'm reading.**

Every day **I watch** TV.

Right now **I'm watching** TV.

Circle the correct word.

1. Every day I ((iron) ironing).

2. Right now I'm (study   studying).

3. Every day I (eat   eating).

4. Right now I'm (go   going) to work.

5. Right now I'm (listen   listening) to music.

6. Every day I (do   doing) the laundry.

7. Right now I'm (feed   feeding) the baby.

8. Every day I (exercise   exercising).

9. Every day I (make   making) breakfast.

10. Right now I'm (play   playing) the guitar.

Listening

Listen and circle *every day* or *right now*.

Example:	You hear: "I study."	You hear: "I'm studying."
	You circle: every day	You circle: right now

1. (every day)   right now
2. every day   right now
3. every day   right now
4. every day   right now

5. every day   right now
6. every day   right now
7. every day   right now
8. every day   right now

Construction Site

I clean the house.

My wife cleans the house.
My husband cleans the house.

Choose

1. I (comb combs) my hair every day.
2. My wife (clean cleans) the house.
3. My husband (wash washes) the dishes.
4. I (eat eats) breakfast.
5. My mother (play plays) the guitar.
6. My father (exercise exercises) every day.
7. I (brush brushes) my teeth every day.
8. My sister (play plays) basketball every day.
9. I (iron irons) every day.
10. My brother (watch watches) TV every day.

Language Experience Journal

My Daily Life

In your Language Experience Journal, write about the things you do every day. Or, tell the story so your teacher can write it. Then read your story to a classmate.

DIFFERENT CULTURES | DIFFERENT WAYS

People in different families share household chores in different ways.

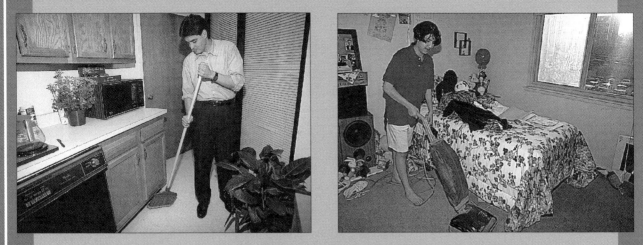

Who does the household chores in your home?

Who makes breakfast? Who makes lunch? Who makes dinner?
Who cleans? Who washes the dishes? Who does the laundry? Who irons?

PUT IT TOGETHER   PART A

INFORMATION GAP ACTIVITY

Work with a partner. First, check (✔) the
things you do every day. Then ask each
other: What do you do every day?
Compare your answers.

You		Your Partner
____	clean	____
____	wash the dishes	____
____	make dinner	____
____	iron	____
____	study	____
____	watch TV	____
____	listen to music	____
____	exercise	____

Do you clean the house every day?

{ Yes, I do.
No, I don't.

INFORMATION GAP ACTIVITY

Work with a partner. First, check (✓) the things you do every day. Then ask each other: What do you do every day? Compare your answers.

You   **Your Partner**

You		Your Partner
____	clean	____
____	wash the dishes	____
____	make dinner	____
____	iron	____
____	study	____
____	watch TV	____
____	listen to music	____
____	exercise	____

Do you clean the house every day?

{ Yes, I do.
No, I don't.

Vocabulary Foundations

get up	make breakfast
take a shower	make lunch
brush teeth	make dinner
comb hair	clean
get dressed	wash the dishes
eat breakfast	do the laundry
go to work	iron
go to school	feed the baby
eat lunch	walk the dog
come home	listen to music
cook dinner	study
read	exercise
watch TV	play the guitar
get undressed	play basketball
go to bed	relax

Language Skill Foundations

I can . . .

☐ identify everyday activities

☐ ask about other people's everyday activities

☐ tell about my own everyday activities

☐ sequence everyday activities

☐ give information about my school and my workplace

☐ greet someone on the telephone

☐ tell someone what I'm doing

☐ compare household chores in different cultures

What things do you see in this classroom? What are the people doing?

IS THIS YOUR PEN?

A. Is this your pen?

B. Yes, it is. Thank you.

A. Is this your pen?

B. No, it isn't.

Practice conversations with a partner.

A. Is this your _____?

B. Yes, it is. Thank you.

A. Is this your _____?

B. No, it isn't.

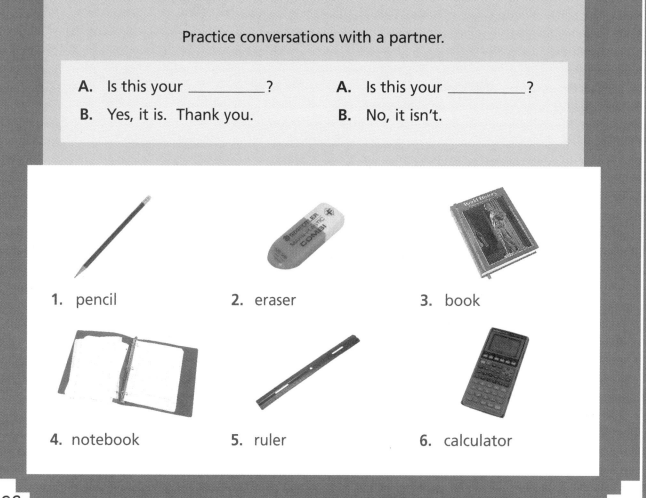

1. pencil

2. eraser

3. book

4. notebook

5. ruler

6. calculator

TALK AND POINT

A. **Where's the bookshelf?**
B. **Over there.**

Practice conversations with a partner.

A. Where's the _____?
B. Over there.

1. desk

2. board

3. chalk

4. bulletin board

5. map

6. globe

7. TV

8. computer

9. overhead projector

29

Matching

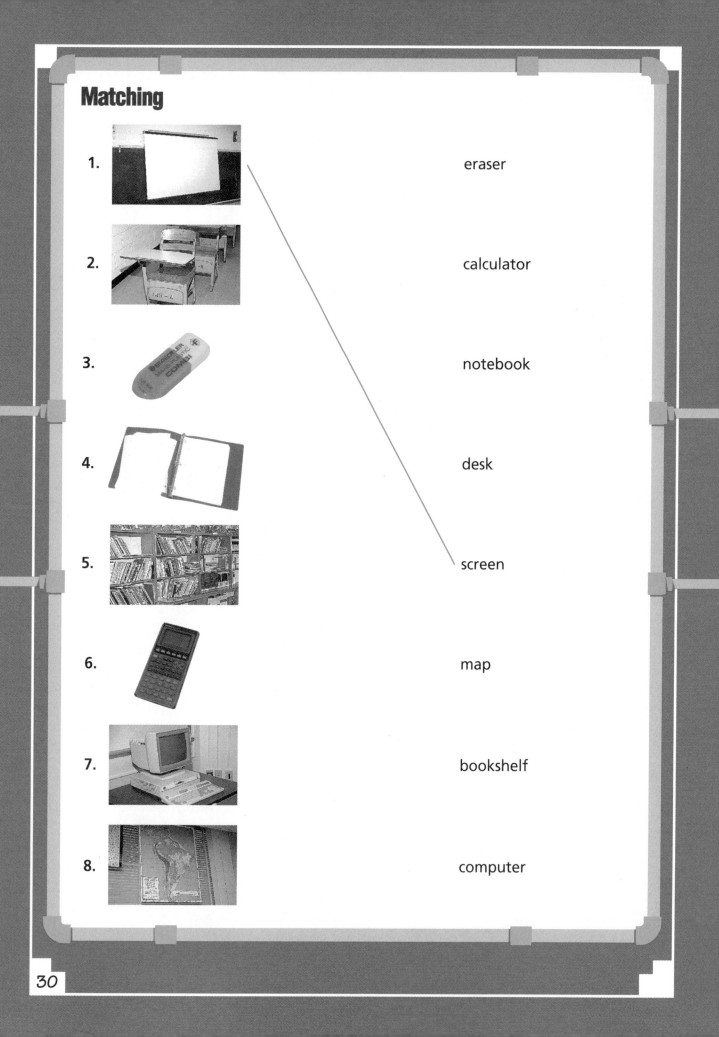

1.   eraser

2.   calculator

3.   notebook

4.   desk

5.   screen

6.   map

7.   bookshelf

8.   computer

Listening

Listen and put a check under the classroom word you hear.

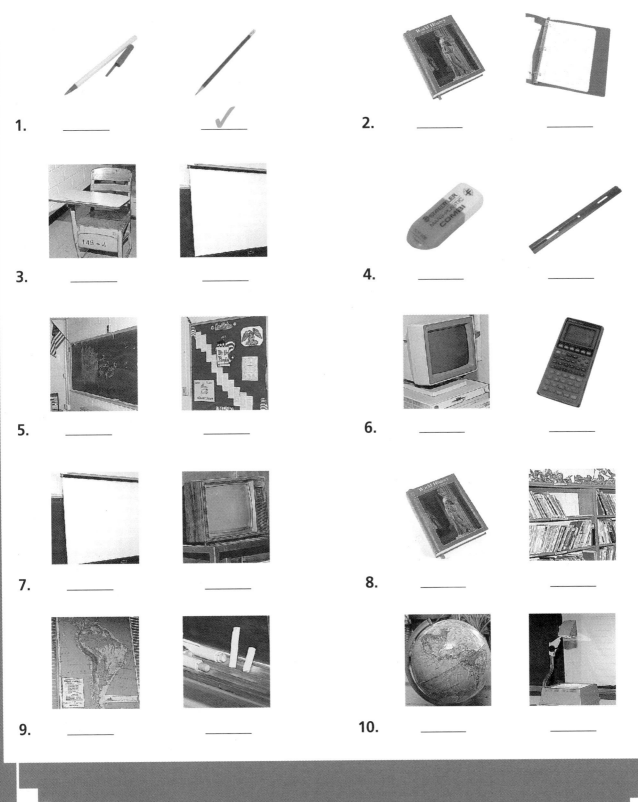

1. _____   ✓_____

2. _____   _____

3. _____   _____

4. _____   _____

5. _____   _____

6. _____   _____

7. _____   _____

8. _____   _____

9. _____   _____

10. _____   _____

Where Are They?

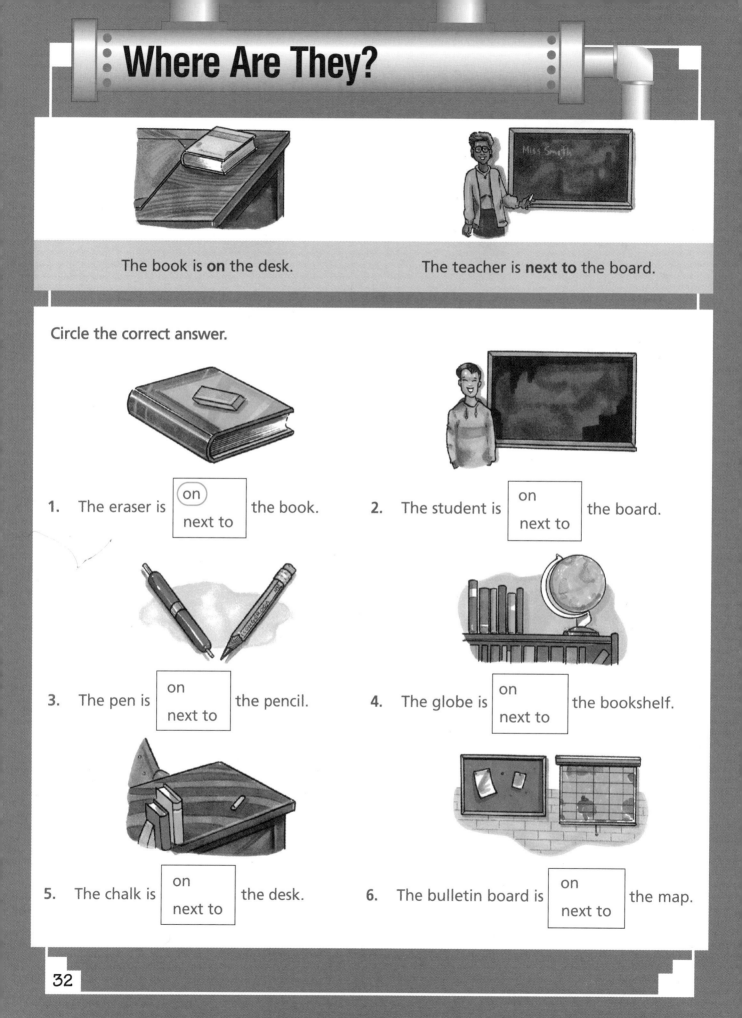

The book is **on** the desk.

The teacher is **next to** the board.

Circle the correct answer.

1. The eraser is (on) / next to the book.

2. The student is on / next to the board.

3. The pen is on / next to the pencil.

4. The globe is on / next to the bookshelf.

5. The chalk is on / next to the desk.

6. The bulletin board is on / next to the map.

Construction Site

There's **a** pencil on my desk.

There's **an** eraser on my desk.

There are pencil**s** on my desk.

There are eraser**s** on my desk.

Fill in the correct word.

a	an	are

1. There's ___a___ TV in my classroom.
2. There ___are___ desks in my classroom.
3. There's _____ bookshelf in my classroom.
4. There's _____ overhead projector in my classroom.
5. There _____ calculators in my classroom.
6. There's _____ computer in my classroom.
7. There _____ bulletin boards in my classroom.

There's	There are

8. ___There's___ a screen in my classroom.
9. ___There are___ books in my classroom.
10. _____ a board in my classroom.
11. _____ a teacher in my classroom.
12. _____ rulers in my classroom.
13. _____ a map in my classroom.
14. _____ students in my classroom.

33

Memory Game

Stand in a circle. Repeat the things you hear.
Add something new.

COMMUNITY CONNECTIONS

Visit another classroom — in your school, in your child's school, or in another school. Make a list of all the things in the classroom. How is it the same as your classroom? How is it different?

Language Experience Journal

My Classroom

In your Language Experience Journal, write about your classroom. Or, describe it so your teacher can write about it. Then read your description to a classmate.

Classroom Actions

Stand up.

Go to the board.

Write your name.

Erase your name.

Sit down.

Open your book.

Read.

Raise your hand.

Give the answer.

Close your book.

35

Matching

1. Stand   your book.
2. Sit   your name.
3. Close   down.
4. Write   up.

5. Erase   your book.
6. Go to   your hand.
7. Open   your name.
8. Raise   the board.

Listening

Listen and write the number under the correct picture.

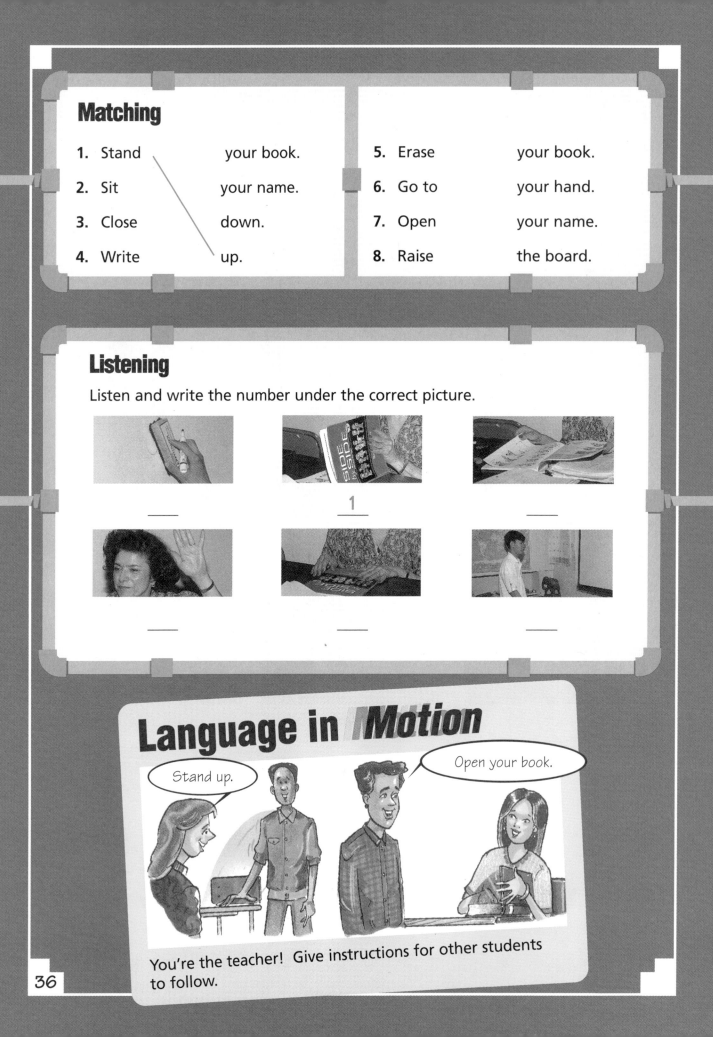

_____   1   _____

_____   _____   _____

Language in Motion

Stand up.

Open your book.

You're the teacher! Give instructions for other students to follow.

Classrooms are different around the world.

Tell about classrooms in other countries.
How are they different from classrooms here?

PUT IT TOGETHER

PART A

INFORMATION GAP ACTIVITY

Work with a partner. You're in two different classrooms. Ask each other about items in your classrooms.

> Is there a bulletin board in your classroom?

> Yes, there is. Is there a bulletin board in YOUR classroom?

> No, there isn't.

Your Classroom		*Your Partner's Classroom*
No	bulletin board	Yes
Yes	map	____
No	bookshelf	____
Yes	TV	____
No	globe	____
Yes	screen	____
No	overhead projector	____
Yes	computer	____

PUT IT TOGETHER PART B

Work with a partner. You're in two different classrooms. Ask each other about items in your classrooms.

Is there a bulletin board in your classroom?

Yes, there is. Is there a bulletin board in YOUR classroom?

No, there isn't.

Your Classroom		Your Partner's Classroom
Yes	bulletin board	No
No	map	___
Yes	bookshelf	___
No	TV	___
Yes	globe	___
No	screen	___
No	overhead projector	___
Yes	computer	___

Vocabulary Foundations

pen
pencil
eraser
book
notebook
ruler
calculator
chalk
teacher
student
desk
board
bulletin board
map
globe
bookshelf
TV
overhead projector
screen
computer

stand up
sit down
write
erase
open
close
read
raise
hand
give
answer
go

Language Skill Foundations

I can . . .

- [ ] identify classroom items
- [ ] ask about someone's possessions
- [ ] express gratitude
- [ ] ask about location
- [ ] tell the location
- [ ] describe my classroom
- [ ] compare classrooms in different cultures
- [ ] follow classroom instructions
- [ ] give classroom instructions

Where are these people? What are they doing?

TELL ME ABOUT THE APARTMENT

A. Tell me about the apartment.

B. It has a very nice living room.

Practice conversations with a partner.

A. Tell me about the apartment.

B. It has a very nice _____.

1. dining room

2. kitchen

3. bedroom

4. bathroom

5. balcony

6. patio

IS THERE A REFRIGERATOR IN THE KITCHEN?

A. Is there a refrigerator in the kitchen?

B. Yes, there is.

Practice conversations with a partner.

A. Is there a _____ in the _____?
B. Yes, there is.

1. fireplace
   living room

2. shower
   bathroom

3. closet
   bedroom

4. stove
   kitchen

5. window
   dining room

Write the Words

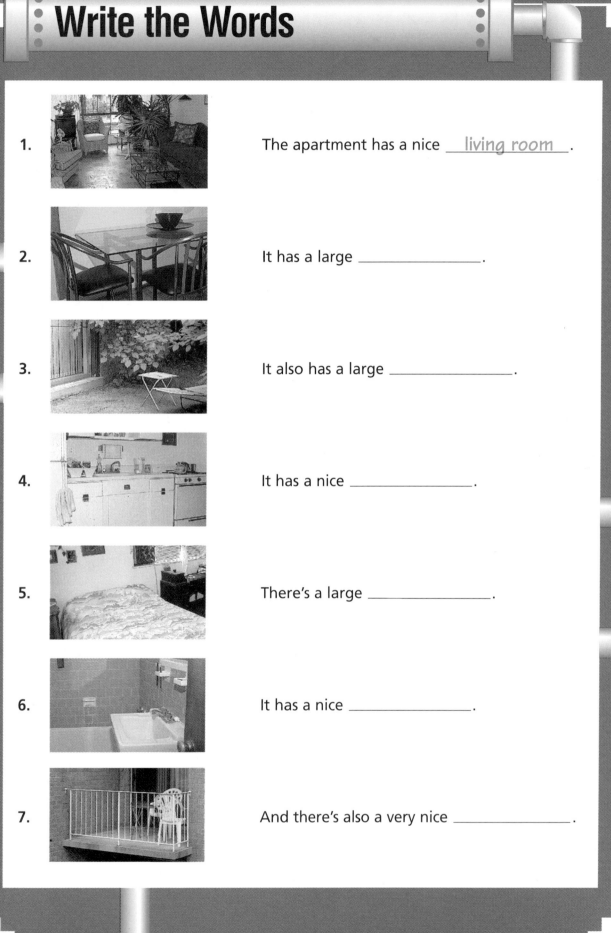

1. The apartment has a nice <u>living room</u>.

2. It has a large _____.

3. It also has a large _____.

4. It has a nice _____.

5. There's a large _____.

6. It has a nice _____.

7. And there's also a very nice _____.

Listening

Listen and put a check under the word you hear.

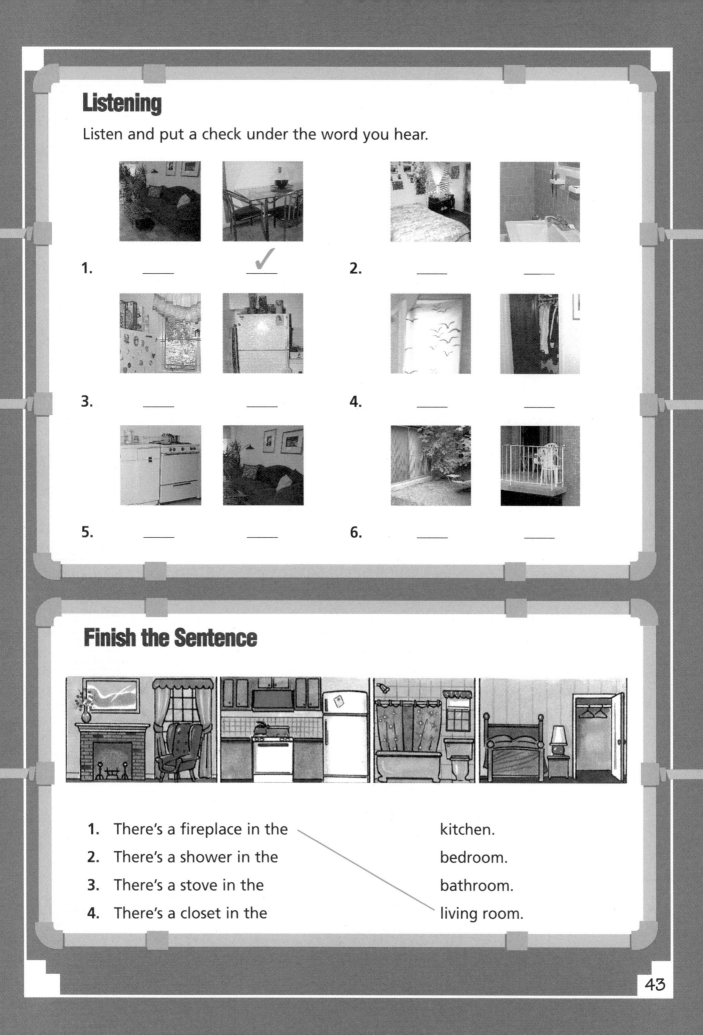

1. ____ ✓   2. ____ ____

3. ____ ____   4. ____ ____

5. ____ ____   6. ____ ____

Finish the Sentence

1. There's a fireplace in the   kitchen.
2. There's a shower in the   bedroom.
3. There's a stove in the   bathroom.
4. There's a closet in the   living room.

WHERE DO YOU WANT THIS TABLE?

A. Where do you want this table?

B. Put it in the dining room.

Practice conversations with a partner.

A. Where do you want this _____?

B. Put it _____.

1. sofa

2. chair

3. bed

4. lamp

5. picture

6. rug

Listening

Listen and put a check under the word you hear.

1. _____ ✓

2. _____ _____

3. _____ _____

4. _____ _____

5. _____ _____

6. _____ _____

Memory ? Game

In my house, there's a table in the kitchen.

In my house, there's a table in the kitchen and a bed in the bedroom.

In my house, there's a table in the kitchen, a bed in the bedroom, and a rug in the dining room.

Stand in a circle. Repeat the things you hear. Add something new.

Missing Letters

1.  re f ri g er a t o r

2. _ l o _ e t

3. f _ r _ p _ a c _

4. _ t _ v e

5. p _ c _ u _ e

6. _ h a _ _

7. _ i _ d o _

8. _ h o _ _ r

9. _ _ _

10. l _ _ _

Language in Motion

You're in the bedroom!

Pantomime an activity at home. Other students guess the room you're in.

DIFFERENT CULTURES | DIFFERENT WAYS

People around the world live in many different kinds of homes.

In your country, what kind of homes do people live in?
Describe a typical home.
How are these homes different from homes here?

COMMUNITY CONNECTIONS

You want to rent an apartment.   You want to rent or buy a house.

Who do you talk to? Find the name, address, and telephone number of a realtor in your community.

Realtor: _____

Address: _____

Telephone Number: _____

My Apartment

I live in a very nice apartment building.

There are three floors in the building.

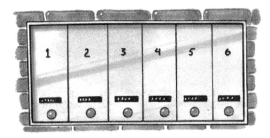

There are six apartments in the building.

There are four rooms in my apartment.

My apartment has a large living room. There are three windows in the living room.

There are two closets in the bedroom.

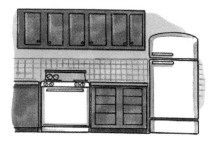

The kitchen is very nice. There's a stove, there's a refrigerator, and there are six cabinets.

I really like my apartment!

What's the Answer?

Answer these questions about the apartment on page 48.

1. How many floors are there in the building?   *There are three floors.*
2. How many apartments are there in the building?   _____
3. How many rooms are there in the apartment?   _____
4. How many windows are there in the living room?   _____
5. How many closets are there in the bedroom?   _____
6. How many cabinets are there in the kitchen?   _____

Language Experience Journal

My Home

In your Language Experience Journal, write about your home. Or, describe it so your teacher can write about it. Then read your description to a classmate.

PUT IT TOGETHER   PART A

INFORMATION GAP ACTIVITY

Work with a partner. You each have different information about the same apartment. Ask each other about the following:

refrigerator in the kitchen   Yes

shower in the bathroom   **No**

fireplace in the living room   **Yes**

stove in the kitchen   _____

closet in the bedroom   _____

window in the dining room   **Yes**

Is there a refrigerator in the kitchen?

Yes, there is.

Work with a partner. You each have different information about the same apartment. Ask each other about the following:

refrigerator in the kitchen	**Yes**
shower in the bathroom	____
fireplace in the living room	____
stove in the kitchen	**No**
closet in the bedroom	**Yes**
window in the dining room	____

Is there a refrigerator in the kitchen?

Yes, there is.

Vocabulary Foundations

living room
dining room
kitchen
bedroom
bathroom
balcony
patio
refrigerator
fireplace
shower
closet
stove
window
table
sofa
chair
bed
lamp
picture
rug

Language Skill Foundations

I can . . .

- [ ] identify rooms in the home
- [ ] ask about an apartment
- [ ] describe features of an apartment
- [ ] identify furniture items
- [ ] identify the name, address, and telephone number of a realtor in my community
- [ ] compare different types of housing around the world

What's happening? What are these people saying to each other?
How are they using numbers?

Cardinal Numbers

1	one
2	two
3	three
4	four
5	five
6	six
7	seven
8	eight
9	nine
10	ten
11	eleven
12	twelve
13	thirteen
14	fourteen
15	fifteen
16	sixteen
17	seventeen
18	eighteen
19	nineteen
20	twenty
21	twenty-one
22	twenty-two
30	thirty
40	forty
50	fifty
60	sixty
70	seventy
80	eighty
90	ninety
100	one hundred

A. **How much is nine plus six?**

B. **Nine plus six is fifteen.**

Practice more addition problems with a partner.

A.   How much is _____ plus _____?

B.   _____ plus _____ is _____.

Listening

Listen and circle the number you hear.

1. 5   (9)
2. 13   15
3. 8   18
4. 20   90
5. 50   60
6. 21   91
7. 90   9
8. 17   70
9. 44   14
10. 69   96

Matching

Match the words and numbers.

1. fifteen   56
2. fifty   14
3. eighty   65
4. eighteen   80
5. forty   15
6. fourteen   38
7. fifty-six   40
8. sixty-five   18
9. eighty-three   50
10. thirty-eight   83

Language in Motion

How much is four plus thirteen?

Four plus thirteen is seventeen.

Move around the classroom. Ask other students addition problems.

It's one o'clock.

It's one fifteen.

It's one thirty.

It's one forty-five.

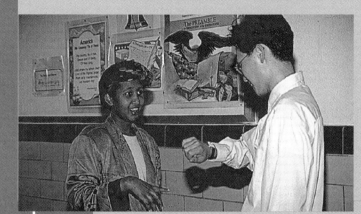

A. **What time is it?**
B. **It's one o'clock.**

Practice conversations with a partner.

A. What time is it?
B. It's _____.

1.

2.

3.

4.

5.

6.

7.

8.

9.

What's the Time?

Circle the correct time.

1. (ten o'clock)   eleven o'clock

2. two fifteen   two thirty

3. eight thirty   eight forty-five

4. nine o'clock   eleven forty-five

5. six o'clock   twelve o'clock

Listening

Listen and circle the time you hear.

1. (6:00)   6:30   4. 10:30   2:30

2. 2:00   4:00   5. 11:00   7:00

3. 5:30   9:30   6. 3:00   3:30

What Time Is It?

Write the time under the clock.

9:00   _____   _____   _____   _____

DAYS OF THE WEEK

Sunday	Monday	Tuesday	Wednesday	Thursday	Friday	Saturday
3	4	5	6	7	8	9

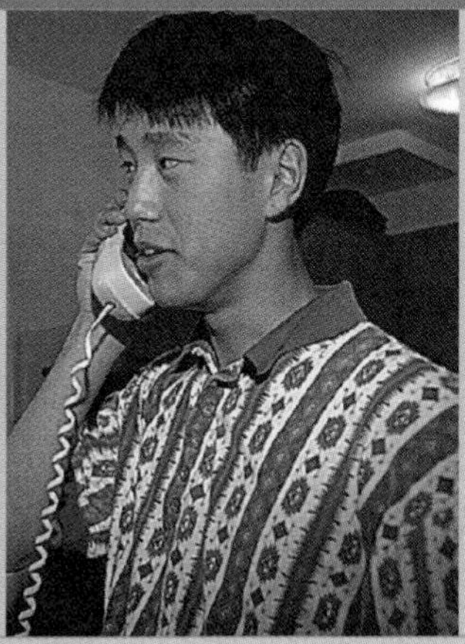

A. Can you come in on Monday at 9:00?

B. On Monday at 9:00? Yes, I can.

Monday
9:00

Practice conversations with a partner.

A. Can you come in on _____ at _____?

B. On _____ at _____? Yes, I can.

Tuesday
5:00

1.

Wednesday
10:15

2.

Thursday
3:30

3.

Friday
11:45

4.

Saturday
2:30

5.

Sunday
12:15

6.

Missing Days

Fill in the missing days.

1. Monday _Tuesday_ Wednesday
2. Thursday _____ Saturday
3. Sunday _____ Tuesday
4. Tuesday _____ Thursday
5. Wednesday _____ Friday
6. Friday _____ Sunday

Listening

Listen and write the time on the calendar.

Monday	Tuesday	Wednesday	Thursday	Friday
			2:00	

Language Experience Journal

My Daily Schedule

In your Language Experience Journal, write about your daily schedule.

When do you get up?
When do you eat breakfast?
When do you go to school or work?
When do you eat lunch?
When do you come home?
When do you eat dinner?
When do you go to bed?

Or, describe your schedule so your teacher can write about it. Then read your story to a classmate.

Ordinal Numbers

1st	first
2nd	second
3rd	third
4th	fourth
5th	fifth
6th	sixth
7th	seventh
8th	eighth
9th	ninth
10th	tenth
11th	eleventh
12th	twelfth
13th	thirteenth
14th	fourteenth
15th	fifteenth
16th	sixteenth
17th	seventeenth
18th	eighteenth
19th	nineteenth
20th	twentieth
21st	twenty-first
22nd	twenty-second
30th	thirtieth
40th	fortieth
50th	fiftieth
60th	sixtieth
70th	seventieth
80th	eightieth
90th	ninetieth
100th	one hundredth

A. **What floor do you live on?**

B. **I live on the twenty-first floor.**

Practice conversations with a partner.

A. What floor do you live on?

B. I live on the _____ floor.

Matching

Match the words and numbers.

1.	fifteenth	22nd
2.	first	15th
3.	fifth	4th
4.	twenty-second	1st
5.	sixteenth	70th
6.	thirty-first	14th
7.	twenty-third	46th
8.	thirtieth	31st
9.	seventieth	5th
10.	forty-sixth	23rd
11.	fourteenth	16th
12.	fourth	30th

Listening

Listen and circle the number you hear.

1.	14th	(13th)		6.	22nd	27th
2.	21st	25th		7.	12th	20th
3.	1st	3rd		8.	1st	30th
4.	26th	21st		9.	13th	30th
5.	80th	8th		10.	14th	44th

MONTHS OF THE YEAR

January	February	March	April	May	June

July	August	September	October	November	December

A. **What month is it?**

B. **It's January.**

A. **Thanks.**

Practice conversations with a partner.

A. What month is it?

B. It's _____.

A. Thanks.

DATES

A. When is your birthday?

B. My birthday is June 9th.

June 9

Practice conversations with a partner.

A. When is your birthday?

B. My birthday is _____.

1. September 19
2. December 10
3. February 6
4. August 15

Memory Game

Walk around the room. Ask students their birthdays. Try to remember the dates.

When is your birthday?

My birthday is November 16th.

Now say all the birthdays. How many did you remember?

WHAT'S TODAY'S DATE?

What's today's date?

MARCH 4 1998

It's March fourth, nineteen ninety-eight.

A. What's today's date?

B. It's _____ _____, _____.
  month   ordinal number   year

61

DIFFERENT CULTURES DIFFERENT WAYS

People in different cultures think of time in different ways.

In your culture, do people arrive on time for work?
Do people arrive on time for appointments?
Do people arrive on time for parties?
Tell about time in your culture.

COMMUNITY CONNECTIONS

Write some important days and times in your daily life.

	Days	Times
I go to work	on _____	from _____ to _____.
I go to school	on _____	from _____ to _____.
My bank is open	on _____	from _____ to _____.
The post office is open	on _____	from _____ to _____.
I take the bus	on _____	at _____.

Important Dates

What are some important dates in your life?

My birthday   _____

My _____'s birthday   _____

My favorite holiday   _____

My first day in this country   _____

Other special dates: _____

_____

PUT IT TOGETHER PART A

Work with a partner. You each have different information about the same train schedule. Ask each other about the following:

Chicago	2:30
Los Angeles	5:45
San Francisco	_____
New York	7:30
Miami	9:00
Boston	_____
Dallas	_____
Toronto	11:15

What time does the train to Chicago leave?

It leaves at 2:30.

Work with a partner. You each have different information about the same train schedule. Ask each other about the following:

Chicago	**2:30**
Los Angeles	_____
San Francisco	**10:00**
New York	_____
Miami	_____
Boston	**3:45**
Dallas	**1:00**
Toronto	_____

What time does the train to Chicago leave?

It leaves at 2:30.

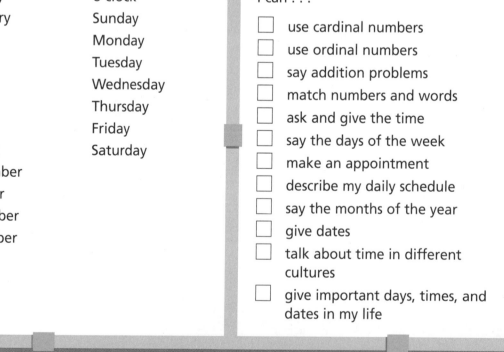

Vocabulary Foundations

January	o'clock
February	Sunday
March	Monday
April	Tuesday
May	Wednesday
June	Thursday
July	Friday
August	Saturday
September	
October	
November	
December	

Language Skill Foundations

I can . . .

- [ ] use cardinal numbers
- [ ] use ordinal numbers
- [ ] say addition problems
- [ ] match numbers and words
- [ ] ask and give the time
- [ ] say the days of the week
- [ ] make an appointment
- [ ] describe my daily schedule
- [ ] say the months of the year
- [ ] give dates
- [ ] talk about time in different cultures
- [ ] give important days, times, and dates in my life

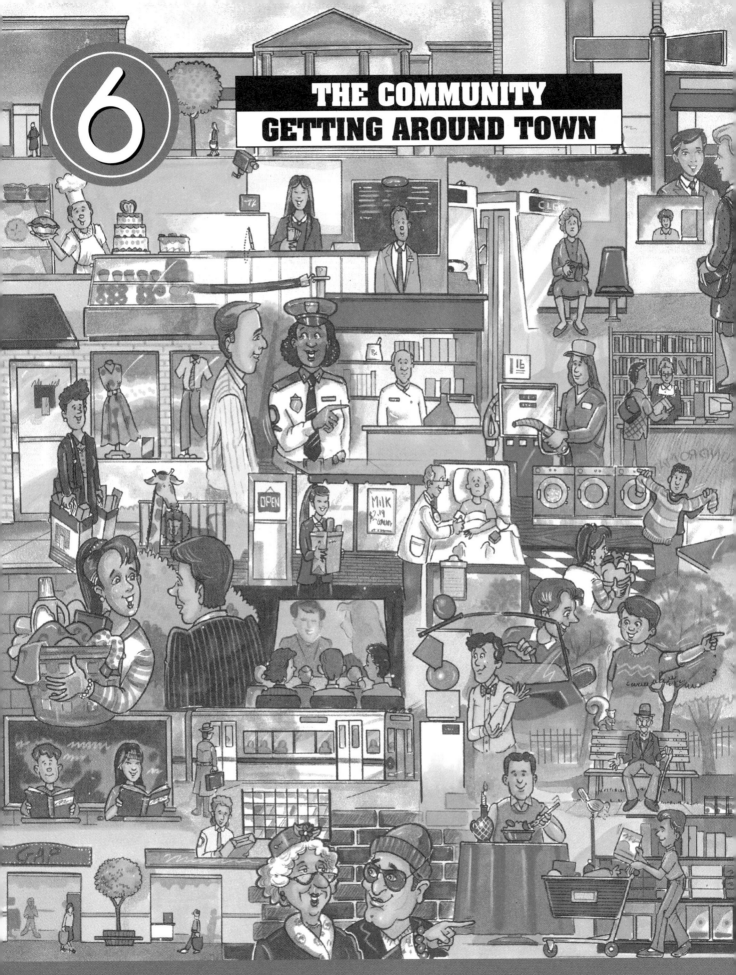

THE COMMUNITY
GETTING AROUND TOWN

What places do you see?
What are people saying to each other?

WHERE ARE YOU GOING?

A. Where are you going?

B. I'm going to the laundromat.

Practice conversations with a partner.

A. Where are you going?

B. I'm going to the _____.

1. drug store

2. bank

3. clinic

4. bakery

5. gas station

6. grocery store

7. bus station

8. department store

9. library

66

Listening

Listen and put a check under the place you hear.

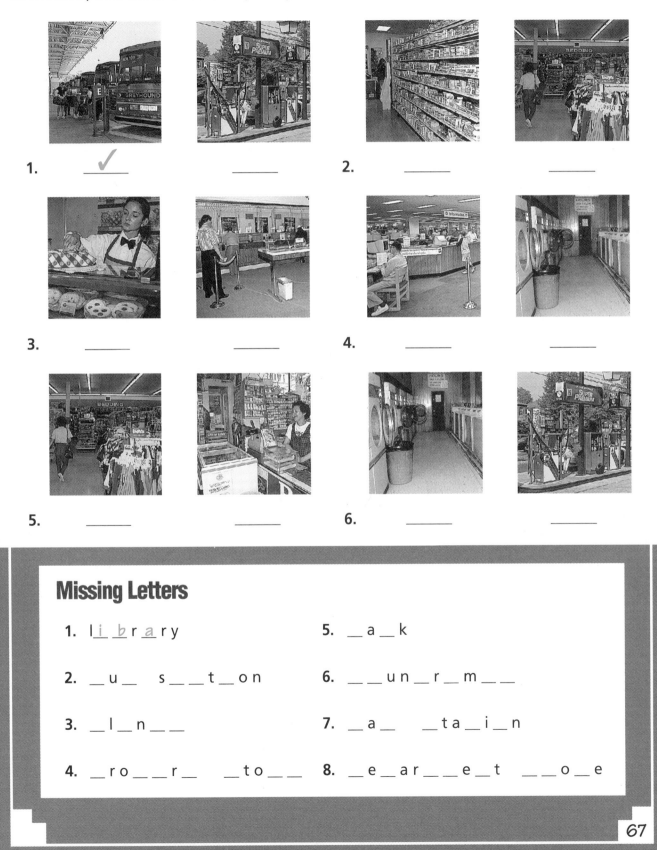

1. _____ ✓   _____   2. _____   _____

3. _____   _____   4. _____   _____

5. _____   _____   6. _____   _____

Missing Letters

1. l i b r a r y

2. _ u _ s _ _ t _ o n

3. _ l _ n _ _

4. _ r o _ _ r _ _ t o _ _

5. _ a _ k

6. _ _ u n _ r _ m _ _ _

7. _ a _ _ t a _ i _ n

8. _ e _ a r _ _ e _ t _ _ o _ e

WHERE'S THE POST OFFICE?

A. Excuse me. Where's the post office?

B. Right over there.

A. Thanks.

Practice conversations with a partner.

A. Excuse me. Where's the _____?

B. Right over there.

A. Thanks.

1. supermarket

2. restaurant

3. park

4. hospital

5. shopping mall

6. movie theater

7. train station

8. museum

9. zoo

Listening

Listen and put a check under the place you hear.

1. <u> ✓ </u>   <u>   </u>

2. <u>   </u>   <u>   </u>

3. <u>   </u>   <u>   </u>

4. <u>   </u>   <u>   </u>

5. <u>   </u>   <u>   </u>

6. <u>   </u>   <u>   </u>

7. <u>   </u>   <u>   </u>

8. <u>   </u>   <u>   </u>

9. <u>   </u>   <u>   </u>

10. <u>   </u>   <u>   </u>

Missing Letters

Fill in the missing letters.

1. <u>p a</u> r <u>k</u>

2. __ __ s __   __ f __ __ c e

3. __ __ p e __ __ a __ __ e __

4. __ e __ __ a __ r __ __ t

5. __ o __ i __   t __ __ a t __ __

6. __ h o __ p __ __ g   __ __ l __

7. __ __ s __ i __ a __

8. __ __ a __ __   __ t __ __ i __ n

Listening

Listen and circle the two places you hear.

1.	(bank)	clinic	(bakery)
2.	park	museum	library
3.	post office	drug store	grocery store
4.	shopping mall	supermarket	laundromat
5.	library	train station	bus station

Memory Game

Today I went to the bank and the supermarket.

Today I went to the bank, the supermarket, and the zoo.

Today I went to the bank.

Stand in a circle. Repeat the places you hear. Add a new place.

WHERE'S THE BANK?

A. **Where's the bank?**

B. **The bank is on Main Street, next to the post office.**

Practice conversations with a partner.

A. Where's the _____?

B. The _____ is on _____, next to the _____.

1. clinic

2. supermarket

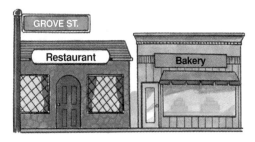

3. movie theater

4. restaurant

WHERE'S THE BUS STATION?

A. Where's the bus station?

B. The bus station is on Central Avenue, across from the shopping mall.

Practice conversations with a partner.

A. Where's the _____?

B. The _____ is on _____, across from the _____.

1. gas station

2. museum

3. library

4. train station

IS THERE A CLINIC NEARBY?

A. Is there a clinic nearby?

B. Yes. There's a clinic on Pine Street, between the super-market and the school.

Practice conversations with a partner.

A. Is there a _____ nearby?

B. Yes. There's a _____ on _____, between the _____ and the _____.

1. bank

2. post office

3. grocery store

4. department store

Street Signs

Look at the pictures. Draw a line.

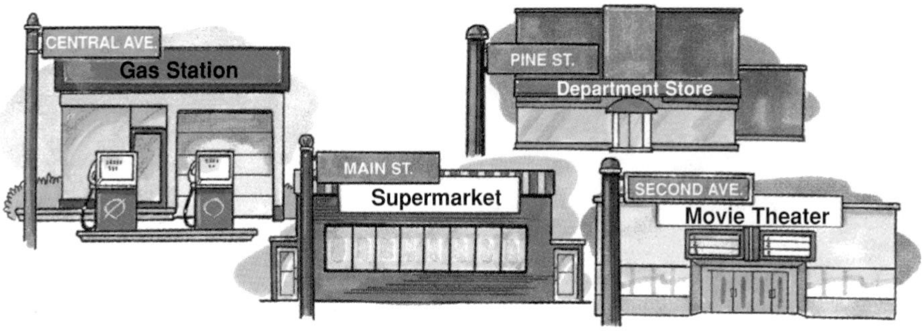

1. gas station — Main Street
2. supermarket — Second Avenue
3. department store — Central Avenue
4. movie theater — Pine Street

Circle the Location

1. (across from)   between
2. between   across from 
3. next to   between 
4. between   next to 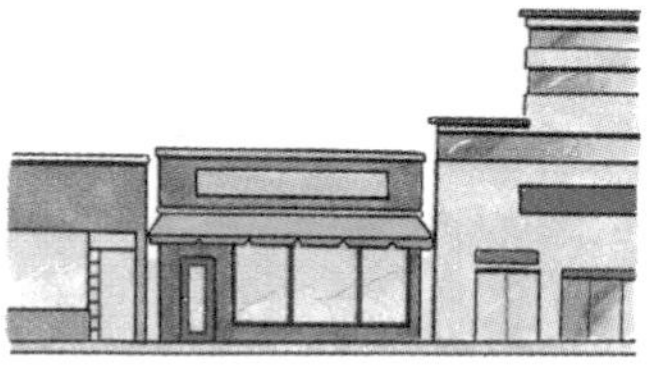
5. across from   next to 
6. between   next to

PART A

INFORMATION GAP ACTIVITY

Work with a partner. You each have a map of the same streets, but your maps have different information. Ask each other questions and fill in the places on your maps.

What's across from the department store?

The gas station.

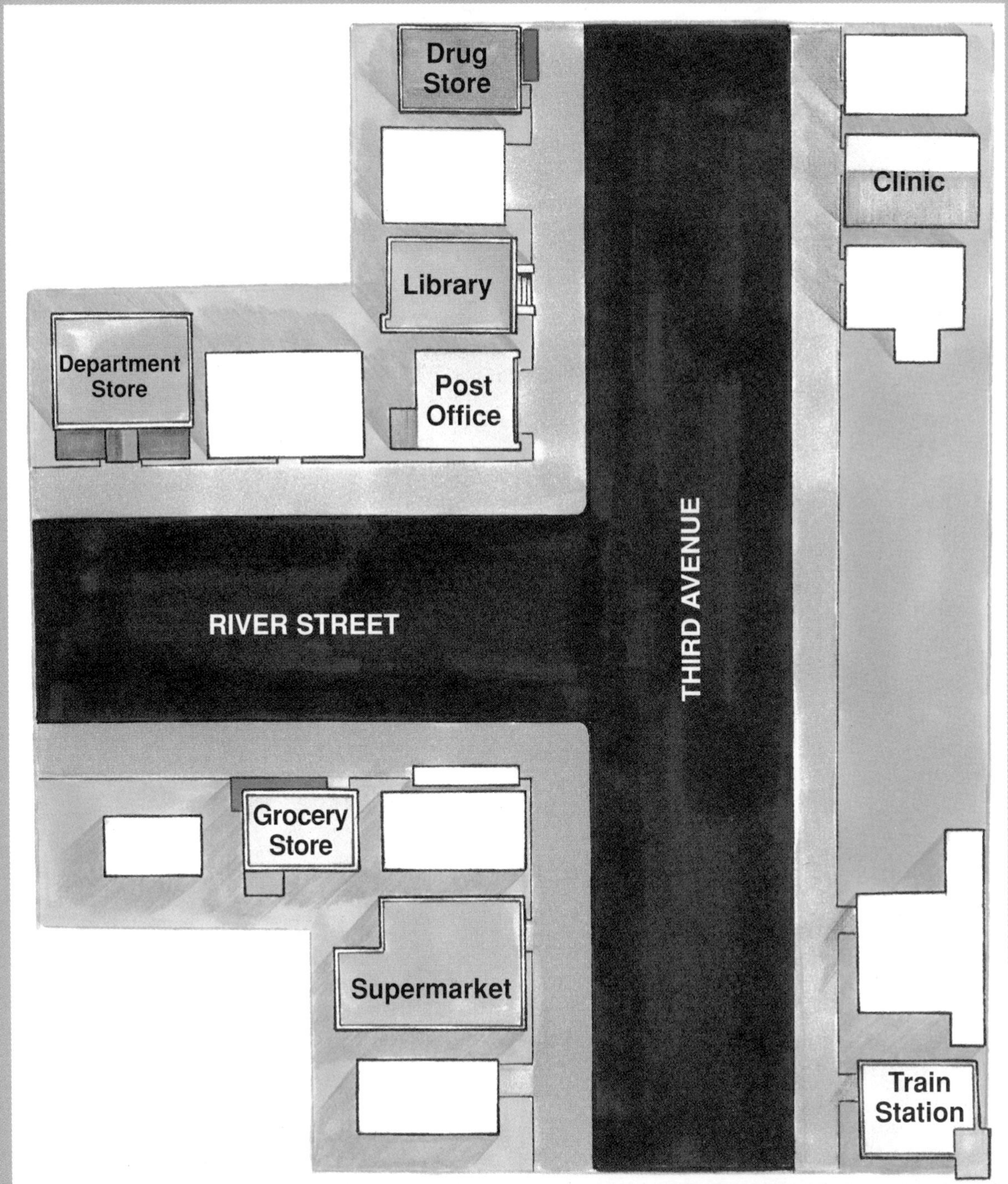

Drug Store

Clinic

Library

Department Store

Post Office

THIRD AVENUE

RIVER STREET

Grocery Store

Supermarket

Train Station

PART **B**

Work with a partner. You each have a map of the same streets, but your maps have different information. Ask each other questions and fill in the places on your maps.

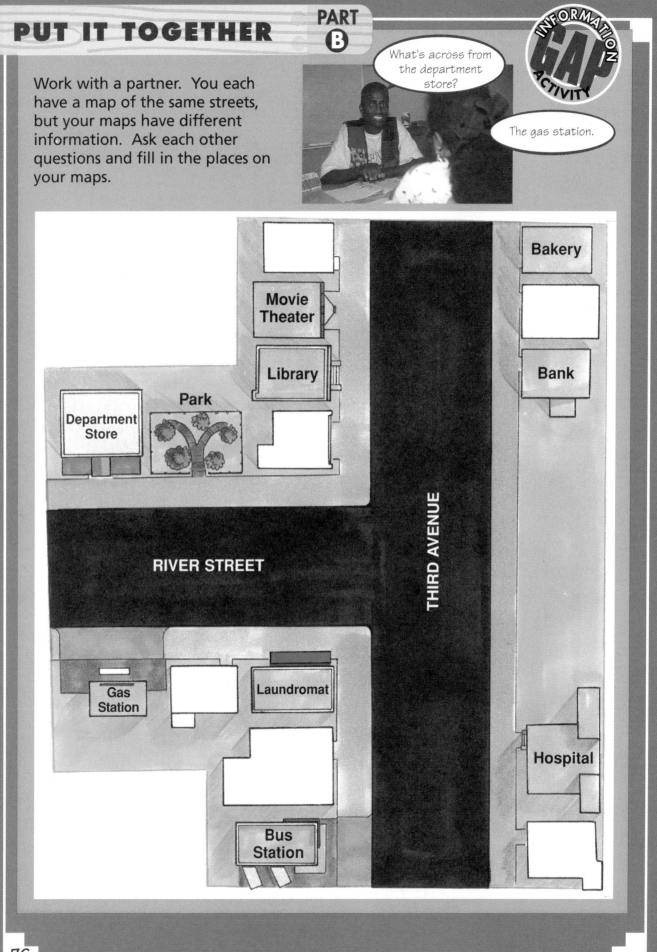

COMMUNITY CONNECTIONS

Fill in the addresses of these places in your community:

bank _____

clinic _____

drug store _____

laundromat _____

library _____

post office _____

supermarket _____

Language in Motion

laundromat

restaurant

Pantomime an activity in a place around town. Other students guess the place.

Language Experience Journal

My Neighborhood

In your Language Experience Journal, write about your neighborhood. Tell about the places in your neighborhood and their locations. Or, describe your neighborhood so your teacher can write about it. Then read your description to a classmate.

DIFFERENT CULTURES | DIFFERENT WAYS

People in different communities shop in different ways.

In many communities people buy their food in large supermarkets and shop in shopping malls. In other communities, people shop in small stores. In some places people shop at markets. Compare places people shop in different communities and different countries.

Vocabulary Foundations

bakery
bank
bus station
clinic
department store
drug store
gas station
grocery store
hospital
laundromat
library
movie theater
museum
park
post office
restaurant
school
shopping mall
supermarket
train station
zoo

next to
across from
between

Language Skill Foundations

I can . . .

☐ identify places in the community

☐ ask for and give the location of places in the community

☐ identify street names

☐ express gratitude

☐ locate places on a map

☐ tell about places in my neighborhood

☐ give the addresses of important places in my community

☐ compare stores in different countries

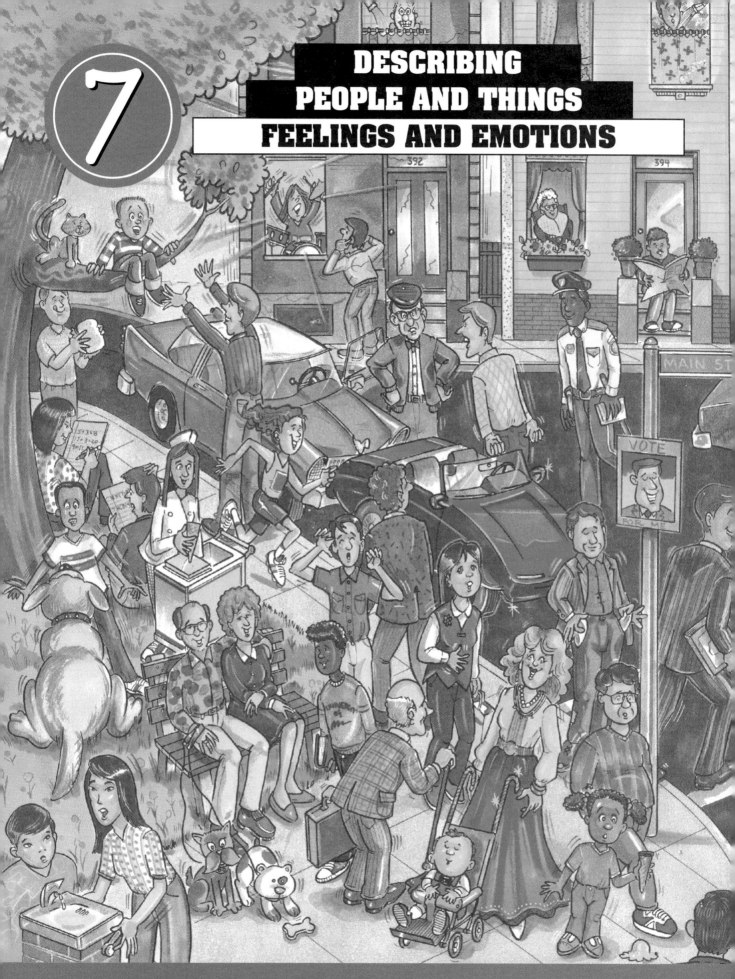

Can you describe these people and things?

Describing People

He's tall.

He's short.

She's young.

She's old.

He's heavy.

He's thin.

She's married.

She's single.

He's rich.

He's poor.

He's handsome.

He's ugly.

She's beautiful.

She's ugly.

A. Is he **tall?**
B. No. He's **short.**

A. Is she **heavy?**
B. No. She's **thin.**

A. Are they **young?**
B. No. They're **old.**

1. thin?

2. old?

3. single?

4. short?

5. poor?

6. handsome?

7. ugly?

8. married?

9. rich?

Listening

Listen and write the number under the correct picture.

_____

_1_

_____

_____

_____

_____

Choose the Correct Word

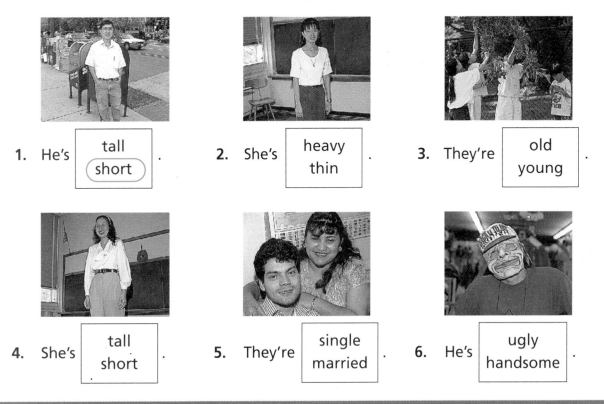

1. He's
| tall |
| short |
.

2. She's
| heavy |
| thin |
.

3. They're
| old |
| young |
.

4. She's
| tall |
| short |
.

5. They're
| single |
| married |
.

6. He's
| ugly |
| handsome |
.

DESCRIBE THESE PEOPLE

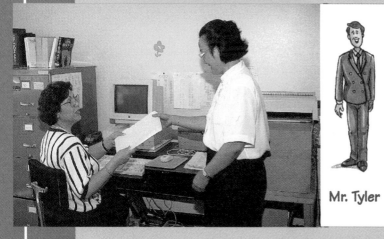

Mr. Tyler

A. Please give this to Mr. Tyler.

B. What does he look like?

A. He's tall, with brown hair.

Practice conversations with a partner.

A. Please give this to _____.

B. What does he/she look like?

A. _____.

Ms. Wilson

George Carter

Mrs. Jackson

1. She's short, with brown hair.

2. He's very tall and thin.

3. She's average height, with curly gray hair.

Mr. Allen

Charlie

Helen Daniels

4. He's short, with straight black hair.

5. He's average height, with gray hair.

6. She's tall, with curly brown hair.

Construction Site

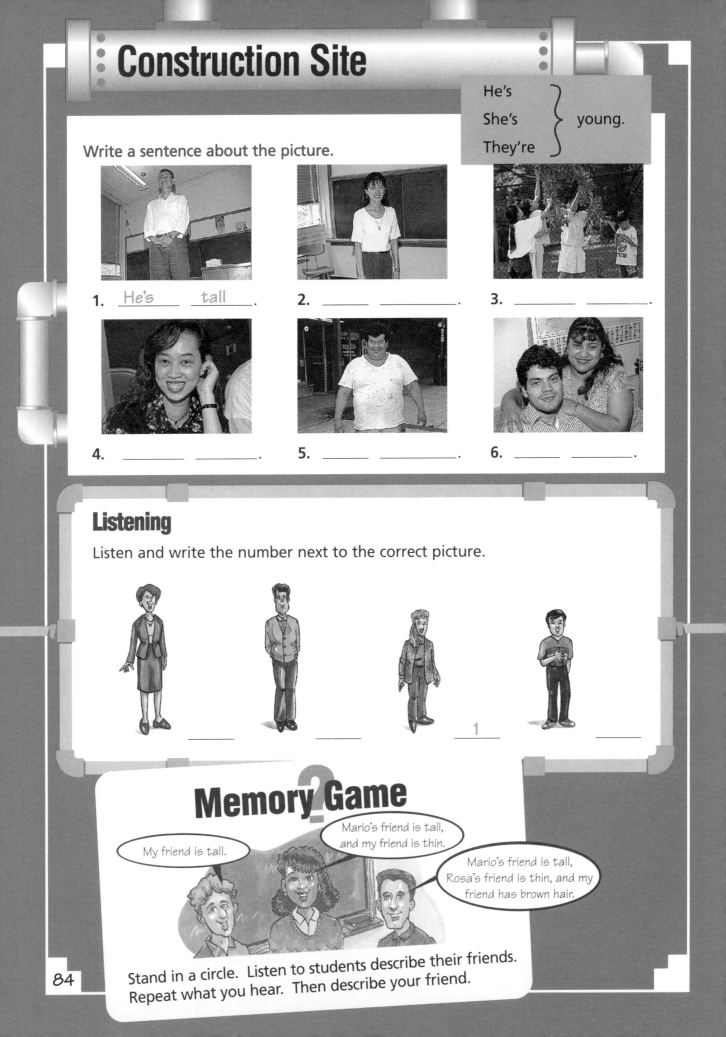

He's
She's } young.
They're

Write a sentence about the picture.

1. _He's_ _tall_ .

2. _____ _____ .

3. _____ _____ .

4. _____ _____ .

5. _____ _____ .

6. _____ _____ .

Listening

Listen and write the number next to the correct picture.

_____   _____   1   _____

Memory Game

My friend is tall.

Mario's friend is tall, and my friend is thin.

Mario's friend is tall, Rosa's friend is thin, and my friend has brown hair.

Stand in a circle. Listen to students describe their friends. Repeat what you hear. Then describe your friend.

DESCRIBING THINGS

A. **Is your car new?**

B. **No. It's old.**

new   old

Practice conversations with a partner.

large   small

1. Is your house _____?

clean   dirty

2. Is the floor _____?

noisy   quiet

3. Is the building _____?

hot   cold

4. Is the water _____?

good   bad

5. Is the food _____?

cheap   expensive

6. Is the restaurant _____?

easy   difficult

7. Is the problem _____?

beautiful   ugly

8. Is the cat _____?

Listening

Listen and circle the word you hear.

1. (old)   cold
2. cheap   clean
3. easy   ugly

4. large   bad
5. beautiful   difficult
6. loud   large

Opposites

1. It isn't large. It's —————————— difficult.
2. It isn't ugly. It's   small.
3. It isn't hot. It's   bad.
4. It isn't clean. It's   beautiful.
5. It isn't easy. It's   cold.
6. It isn't noisy. It's   quiet.
7. It isn't good. It's   dirty.

Missing Letters

1. c _l_ _e_ a _n_
2. _ _ e _ p
3. d _ _ _ i _ u _ t
4. _ _ i e _
5. l _ _ _ e

6. _ m a _ _
7. _ _ r _ y
8. _ a _ y
9. u _ _ _
10. _ e _ u _ _ f _ _

Language in Motion

tall

old

cold

Pantomime an adjective. Other students guess the word.

COMMUNITY CONNECTIONS

Describe your community. What places and things in your community can you describe with these words? Share your list with the class.

large: _____

_____

beautiful: _____

_____

dirty: _____

_____

quiet: _____

_____

noisy: _____

_____

expensive: _____

_____

FEELINGS

A. Are you hungry?
B. Yes. I'm very hungry.

Practice conversations with a partner.

A. Are you _____?
B. Yes. I'm very _____.

1. thirsty

2. tired

3. happy

4. sad

5. sick

6. upset

7. angry

8. nervous

9. afraid

Circle the Word

1. (tired) angry

2. hungry thirsty

3. upset happy

4. afraid sick

5. sad nervous

6. angry hungry

Finish the Sentence

1. When I'm hungry, I   go to the clinic.

2. When I'm sick, I   drink some water.

3. When I'm tired, I   eat dinner.

4. When I'm thirsty, I   go to bed.

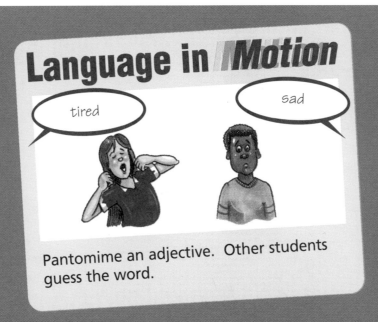

Language in Motion

tired

sad

Pantomime an adjective. Other students guess the word.

Listening

Listen and put a check under the word you hear.

1.　✓　　　_____　　　　2.　_____　_____

3.　_____　_____　　　　4.　_____　_____

5.　_____　_____　　　　6.　_____　_____

Language Experience Journal

Happy Times and Sad Times

In your Language Experience Journal, write about times when you feel happy and times when you feel sad. Or, tell your story so your teacher can write it. Then read your story to a classmate.

People in different cultures show their feelings in different ways.

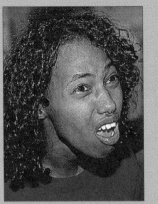
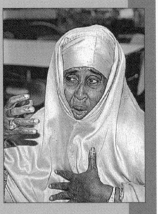

How are these people feeling?
In your culture, how do people show they're happy?
How do people show they're sad?
How do people show they're angry?
How do people show they're nervous?

PUT IT TOGETHER   PART A

INFORMATION GAP ACTIVITY

Work with a partner. You each have different information about the same apartment for rent. Ask each other questions about the apartment.

Is the building new or old?

It's old.

building:	new	old
kitchen:	large	small
apartment:	clean	dirty
building:	noisy	quiet
rent:	cheap	expensive
neighborhood:	beautiful	ugly

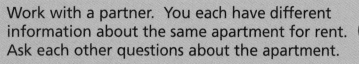

PUT IT TOGETHER — PART B

INFORMATION GAP ACTIVITY

Work with a partner. You each have different information about the same apartment for rent. Ask each other questions about the apartment.

building:	new	(old)
kitchen:	large	small
apartment:	(clean)	dirty
building:	noisy	(quiet)
rent:	cheap	expensive
neighborhood:	beautiful	ugly

> Is the building new or old?

> It's old.

Vocabulary Foundations

tall	large	hungry
short	small	thirsty
young	clean	sick
old	dirty	happy
heavy	noisy	sad
thin	quiet	upset
married	hot	angry
single	cold	nervous
rich	good	afraid
poor	bad	
beautiful	cheap	curly hair
handsome	expensive	straight hair
ugly	easy	black
new	difficult	brown
old	tired	gray

Language Skill Foundations

I can . . .

- [ ] describe people
- [ ] ask what people look like
- [ ] describe things
- [ ] make positive and negative statements
- [ ] describe places and things in my community
- [ ] describe my classroom
- [ ] ask about and express feelings
- [ ] compare how people show their feelings in different cultures

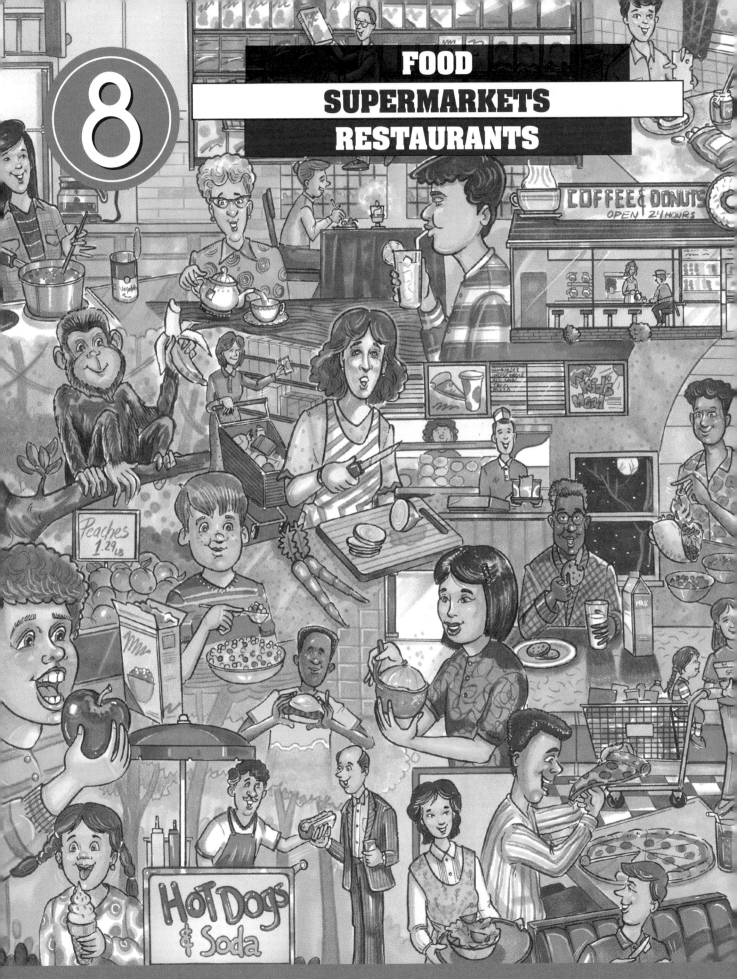

8

FOOD
SUPERMARKETS
RESTAURANTS

What foods do you see?
What are the people saying?

I'M LOOKING FOR A COOKIE

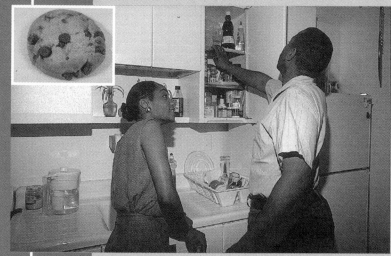

A. **What are you looking for?**

B. **A cookie.**

A. **Sorry. There aren't any more cookies.**

Practice conversations with a partner.

A. What are you looking for?

B. _____.

A. Sorry. There aren't any more _____s.

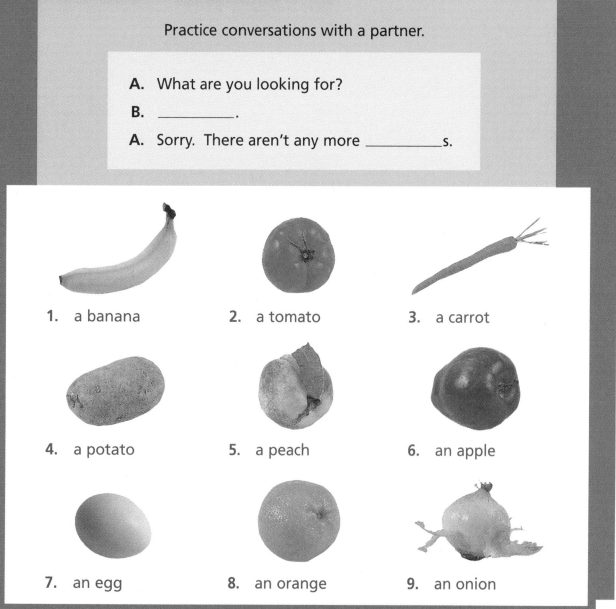

1. a banana

2. a tomato

3. a carrot

4. a potato

5. a peach

6. an apple

7. an egg

8. an orange

9. an onion

Construction Site

Circle the correct word.

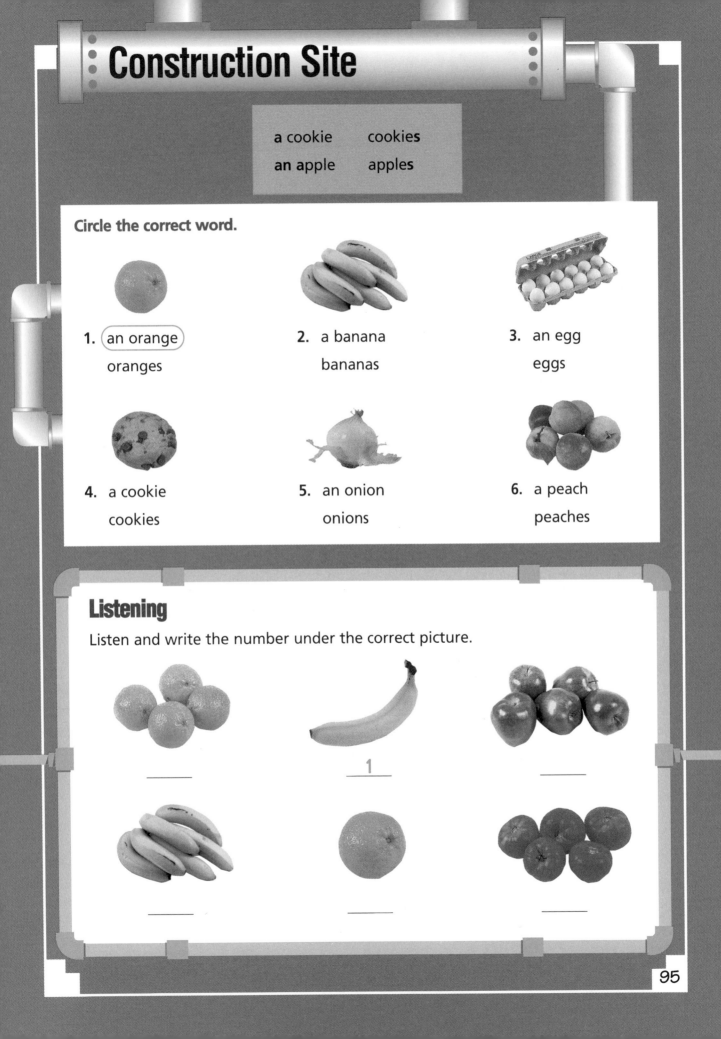

1. (an orange)
   oranges

2. a banana
   bananas

3. an egg
   eggs

4. a cookie
   cookies

5. an onion
   onions

6. a peach
   peaches

Listening

Listen and write the number under the correct picture.

_____   __1__   _____

_____   _____   _____

THERE ISN'T ANY MORE BREAD

A. **What are you looking for?**

B. **Bread.**

A. **Sorry. There isn't any more bread.**

Practice conversations with a partner.

A. What are you looking for?

B. _____.

A. Sorry. There isn't any more _____.

1. milk

2. cheese

3. lettuce

4. ice cream

5. soup

6. cereal

7. soda

8. butter

9. sugar

Listening

Listen and write the number under the correct picture.

_____

_____

1

_____

_____

_____

Circle the Correct Word

1. There isn't any more ((soup) cookies).

2. There aren't any more (onions   milk).

3. There aren't any more (cheese   apples).

4. There isn't any more (ice cream   bananas) .

Memory Game

I'm looking for bread and apples.

I'm looking for bread.

I'm looking for bread, apples, and ice cream.

Stand in a circle. Repeat the foods you hear.
Add a new food.

Food in Your Home

Tell about the food in your home today.

1. Is there any milk?   _____

2. Are there any eggs?   _____

3. Are there any bananas?   _____

4. Is there any bread?   _____

5. Are there any cookies?   _____

Language in Motion

What's your favorite food?

Ice cream.

Walk around the room. Ask all the students about their favorite foods. How many favorite foods can you remember?

Language Experience Journal

My Favorite Food

In your Language Experience Journal, write about your very favorite food. What is it? Why do you like it? When do you eat it? Or, tell about your favorite food so your teacher can write about it. Then read your story to a classmate.

WHAT DO WE NEED?

A. What do we need at the supermarket?

B. We need a box of cookies.

Practice conversations with a partner.

A. What do we need at the supermarket?

B. We need _____.

1. a bag of sugar

2. a bottle of soda

3. a quart of milk

4. a bunch of bananas

5. a can of soup

6. a pound of cheese

7. a jar of mayonnaise

8. a loaf of bread

9. a dozen eggs

Matching

1. jar   cheese
2. bottle   eggs
3. pound   mayonnaise
4. bag   soda
5. dozen   sugar

6. box   milk
7. quart   bananas
8. loaf   soup
9. can   cookies
10. bunch   bread

Listening

Listen and put a check under the foods you hear.

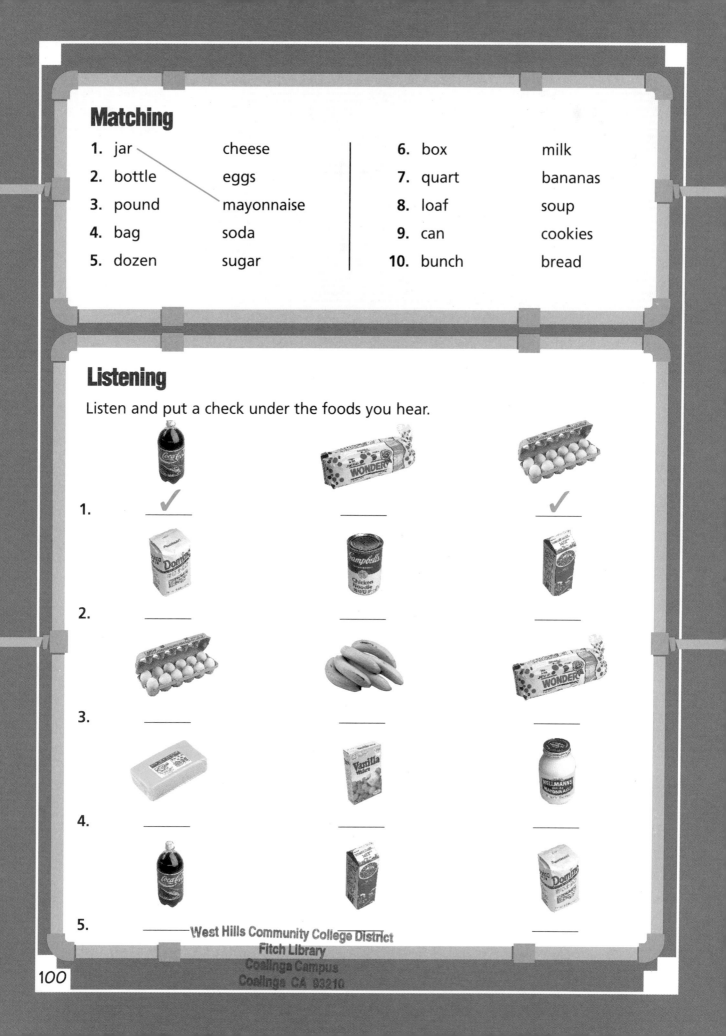

1.   ___✓___   _____   ___✓___

2.   _____   _____   _____

3.   _____   _____   _____

4.   _____   _____   _____

5.   _____   _____   _____

Memory Game

Stand in a circle. Repeat the foods you hear. Add a new food.

A Shopping List

Make a shopping list of all the foods you need to buy at the supermarket.

My Shopping List

Compare your list with other students' lists.

ORDERING FOOD

A. Can I help you?

B. Yes. I'd like a hamburger, please.

Practice conversations with a partner.

A. Can I help you?

B. Yes. I'd like _____, please.

1. a cheeseburger

2. a hot dog

3. a sandwich

4. a taco

5. a pizza

6. a donut

7. coffee

8. tea

9. lemonade

Listening

Listen and put a check under the foods you hear.

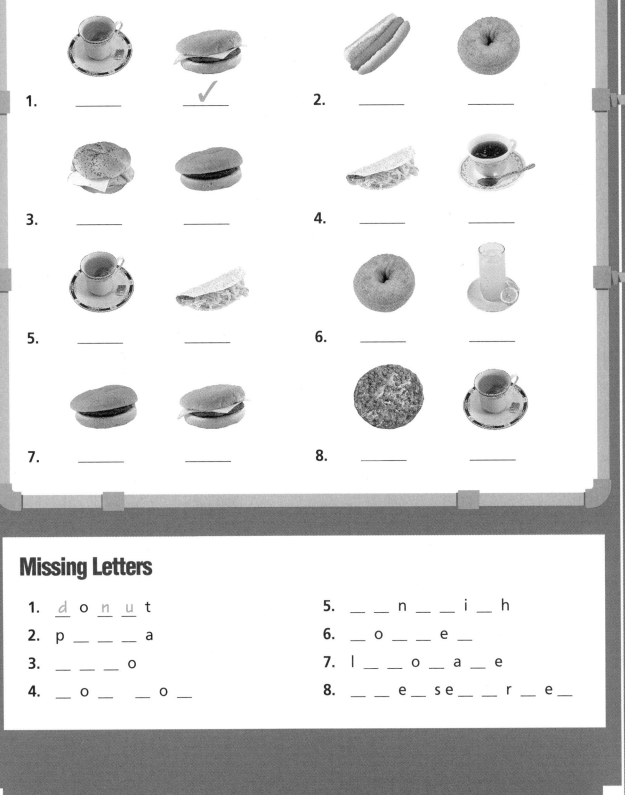

1. _____ _____✓_____ 2. _____ _____

3. _____ _____ 4. _____ _____

5. _____ _____ 6. _____ _____

7. _____ _____ 8. _____ _____

Missing Letters

1. d o n u t
2. p _ _ _ a
3. _ _ _ o
4. _ o _ _ o _
5. _ _ n _ _ i _ h
6. _ o _ _ e _
7. l _ _ o _ a _ e
8. _ _ e _ se _ _ r _ e _

COMMUNITY CONNECTIONS

Where do you buy food? What stores do you recommend? Where are they? Make a list, and discuss with other students.

Store	Location

Do you sometimes go to fast-food restaurants? Where do you go? What foods do you like there? Make a list, and discuss with other students.

Fast-Food Restaurant	Foods

People around the world eat many different kinds of foods.

Tell about foods in your culture.
What do people usually eat for breakfast?
What do people eat for lunch?
What do people eat for dinner?

PUT IT TOGETHER   PART A

INFORMATION GAP ACTIVITY

Work with a partner. What foods do you have in your kitchens? Ask each other about this list of foods.

	You	Your Partner
milk	No	Yes
cookies	Yes	_____
butter	Yes	_____
oranges	No	_____
ice cream	No	_____
eggs	Yes	_____
soda	Yes	_____

Is there any milk in your house?

Yes, there is.

Work with a partner. What foods do you have in your kitchens? Ask each other about this list of foods.

Is there any milk in your house?

Yes, there is.

	You	Your Partner
milk	Yes	_____
cookies	No	_____
butter	Yes	_____
oranges	Yes	_____
ice cream	Yes	_____
eggs	No	_____
soda	Yes	_____

Vocabulary Foundations

apple	lemonade	bag
banana	lettuce	bottle
bread	mayonnaise	box
butter	milk	bunch
carrot	onion	can
cereal	orange	dozen
cheese	peach	loaf
cheeseburger	pizza	jar
coffee	potato	quart
cookie	sandwich	pound
donut	soda	
egg	soup	
hamburger	sugar	
hot dog	taco	
ice cream	tea	
	tomato	

Language Skill Foundations

I can . . .

☐ name common foods

☐ distinguish between *count* and *non-count* food items

☐ express food needs

☐ tell about my favorite foods

☐ identify food containers and quantities

☐ make a shopping list

☐ name common restaurant foods

☐ order food in a restaurant

☐ recommend food stores and restaurants in my community

☐ compare foods and meals in different cultures

9

What clothing do you see?

Colors

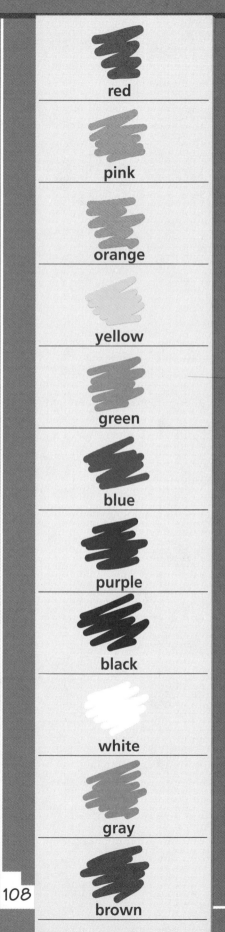

red

pink

orange

yellow

green

blue

purple

black

white

gray

brown

A. What's your favorite color?

B. Blue.

Practice conversations with a partner.

A. What's your favorite color?

B. _____.

Language in Motion

What's your favorite color?

Walk around the room. Ask students about their favorite color. Can you remember everybody's favorite color?

I'M LOOKING FOR A SHIRT

A. I'm looking for a shirt.

B. Shirts are over there.

A. Thank you.

Practice conversations with a partner.

A. I'm looking for _____.

B. _____s are over there.

A. Thank you.

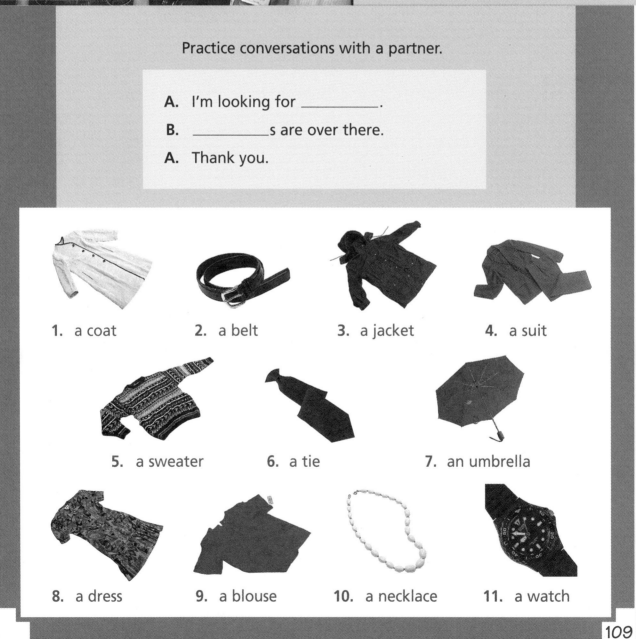

1. a coat **2.** a belt **3.** a jacket **4.** a suit

5. a sweater **6.** a tie **7.** an umbrella

8. a dress **9.** a blouse **10.** a necklace **11.** a watch

Circle the Correct Word

1. coat
   (dress)

2. blouse
   sweater

3. umbrella
   jacket

4. shirt
   coat

5. tie
   suit

6. necklace
   blouse

One or More?

1. sweater
   (sweaters)

2. shirt
   shirts

3. skirt
   skirts

4. blouse
   blouses

5. umbrella
   umbrellas

6. tie
   ties

Write and Say

1. a coat   _coats_
2. a tie   _____
3. a _____   blouses
4. a _____   jackets
5. a sweater   _____
6. a necklace _____
7. an _____   umbrellas
8. a dress   _____

Listening

Listen and put a check under the item of clothing you hear.

1. ___✓___ _____   2. _____ _____

3. _____ _____   4. _____ _____

5. _____ _____   6. _____ _____

Circle the Correct Word

1. I'm looking for a (shirt   shirts).
2. (Dress   Dresses) are over there.
3. I'm looking for a (blouse   blouses).
4. (Tie   Ties) are over there.
5. I'm looking for a blue (suit   suits).
6. Where are (sweater   sweaters)?
7. I'm looking for a (jacket   jackets).
8. Where are (umbrella   umbrellas)?

I'M LOOKING FOR A PAIR OF PANTS

A. May I help you?

B. Yes. I'm looking for a pair of pants.

A. Pants are over there.

Practice conversations with a partner.

A. May I help you?

B. Yes. I'm looking for a pair of _____.

A. _____ are over there.

1. shoes

2. socks

3. jeans

4. pajamas

5. gloves

6. mittens

Listening

Listen and put a check under the item of clothing you hear.

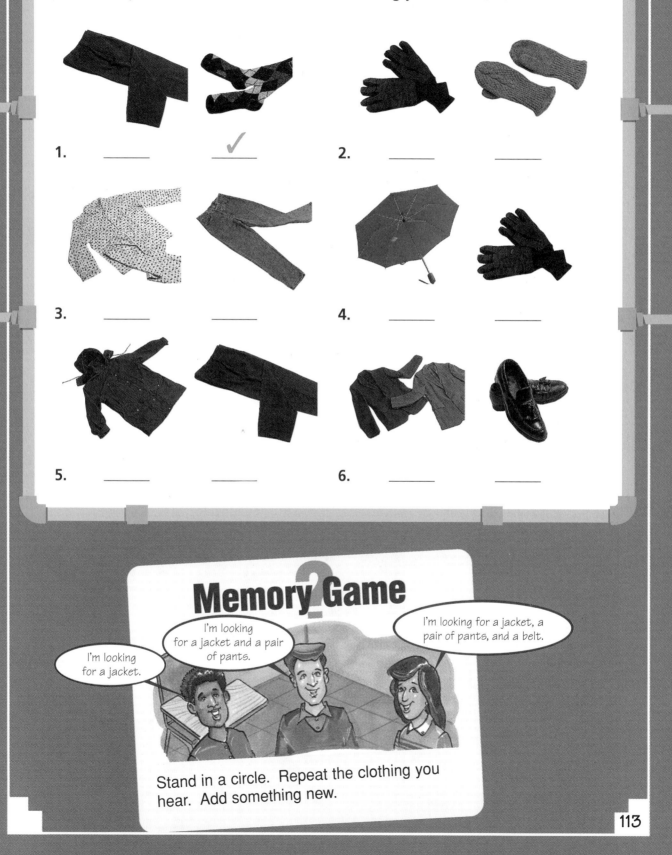

1. _____ ✓_____   2. _____ _____

3. _____ _____   4. _____ _____

5. _____ _____   6. _____ _____

Memory Game

I'm looking for a jacket.

I'm looking for a jacket and a pair of pants.

I'm looking for a jacket, a pair of pants, and a belt.

Stand in a circle. Repeat the clothing you hear. Add something new.

What Are They Wearing?

He's wearing a white _____shirt_____ [1],
black _____ [2], and a gray
_____ [3].

She's wearing a blue _____ [4],
a yellow _____ [5], and orange
_____ [6].

He's wearing a blue_____ [7],
a green _____ [8], and red
_____ [9].

She's wearing a pink _____ [10],
a purple _____ [11], and white
_____ [12].

Guessing Game

Look at the clothing students
are wearing today. Then close
your eyes or look up. Describe
the clothing of another student.
Can your classmates guess which
student you're talking about?

This person is wearing
a blue shirt, black pants,
and brown shoes.

Is it Carlos?

SIZES

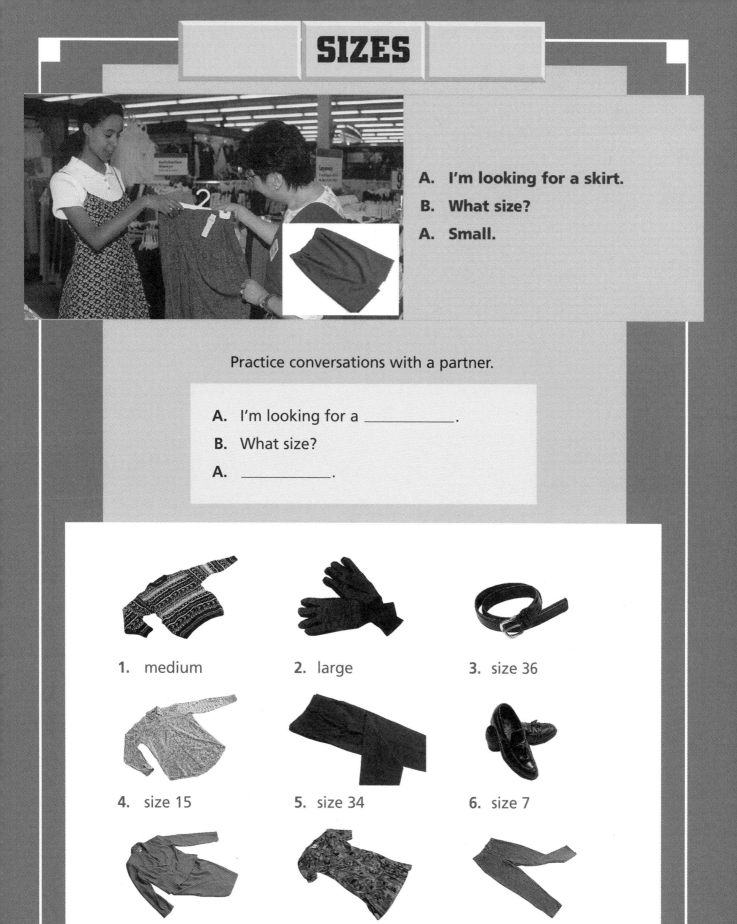

A. I'm looking for a skirt.

B. What size?

A. Small.

Practice conversations with a partner.

A. I'm looking for a _____.

B. What size?

A. _____.

1. medium

2. large

3. size 36

4. size 15

5. size 34

6. size 7

7. size 40

8. size 12

9. size 32

Listening

Listen and circle what you hear.

1. (belt)   blouse
2. sweater   shirt
3. 14   40
4. 34   36

5. green   gray
6. black   blue
7. 8   white
8. medium   green

COMMUNITY CONNECTIONS

Where do you shop for different types of clothing? What stores do you recommend? Where are they? Make a list, and discuss with other students.

Clothing	Store	Location

Language Experience Journal

My Favorite Clothing

In your Language Experience Journal, write about your favorite article of clothing. What is it? What color and size is it? Where is it from? Why do you like it? When do you wear it? Or, tell your story so your teacher can write it. Then read your story to a classmate.

People in different cultures have special clothing for special days.

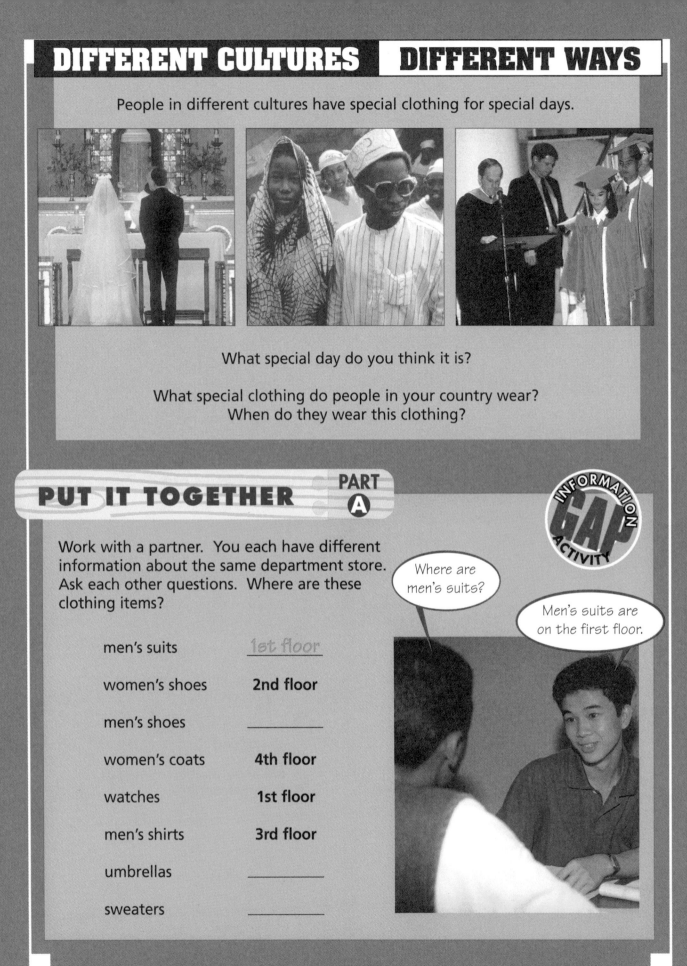

What special day do you think it is?

What special clothing do people in your country wear?
When do they wear this clothing?

PUT IT TOGETHER — PART A

INFORMATION GAP ACTIVITY

Work with a partner. You each have different information about the same department store. Ask each other questions. Where are these clothing items?

Where are men's suits?

Men's suits are on the first floor.

men's suits	1st floor
women's shoes	**2nd floor**
men's shoes	_____
women's coats	**4th floor**
watches	**1st floor**
men's shirts	**3rd floor**
umbrellas	_____
sweaters	_____

Work with a partner. You each have different information about the same department store. Ask each other questions. Where are these clothing items?

men's suits	**1st floor**
women's shoes	_____
men's shoes	**5th floor**
women's coats	_____
watches	_____
men's shirts	_____
umbrellas	**1st floor**
sweaters	**6th floor**

Where are men's suits?

Men's suits are on the first floor.

Vocabulary Foundations

belt	umbrella	size
blouse	watch	small
coat		medium
dress	black	large
gloves	blue	
jacket	brown	
jeans	gray	
mittens	green	
necklace	orange	
pajamas	pink	
pants	purple	
shirt	red	
shoes	white	
skirt	yellow	
socks		
suit		
sweater		
tie		

Language Skill Foundations

I can . . .

- [ ] name colors
- [ ] ask for clothing in a store
- [ ] describe what people are wearing
- [ ] identify clothing sizes
- [ ] recommend clothing stores in my community
- [ ] tell about my favorite article of clothing
- [ ] tell about special clothing in different cultures

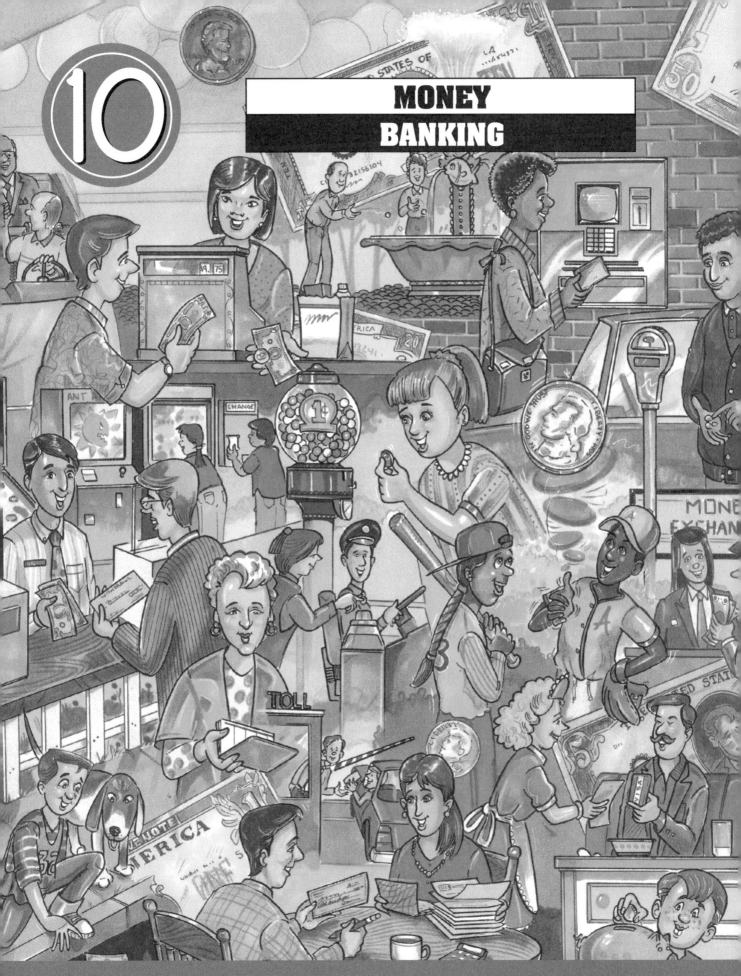

What money do you see?
What are people doing? What are they saying?

Coins

A **penny** is one cent.   1¢   or $.01

A **nickel** is five cents.   5¢   or $.05

A **dime** is ten cents.   10¢   or $.10

A **quarter** is twenty-five cents.   25¢   or $.25

A **half-dollar** is fifty cents.   50¢   or $.50

Look! I just found a quarter!

Practice with other coins.

Look! I just found a _____!

Matching

1. ten cents   penny

2. fifty cents   quarter

3. twenty-five cents   nickel

4. five cents   dime

5. one cent   half-dollar

Amounts

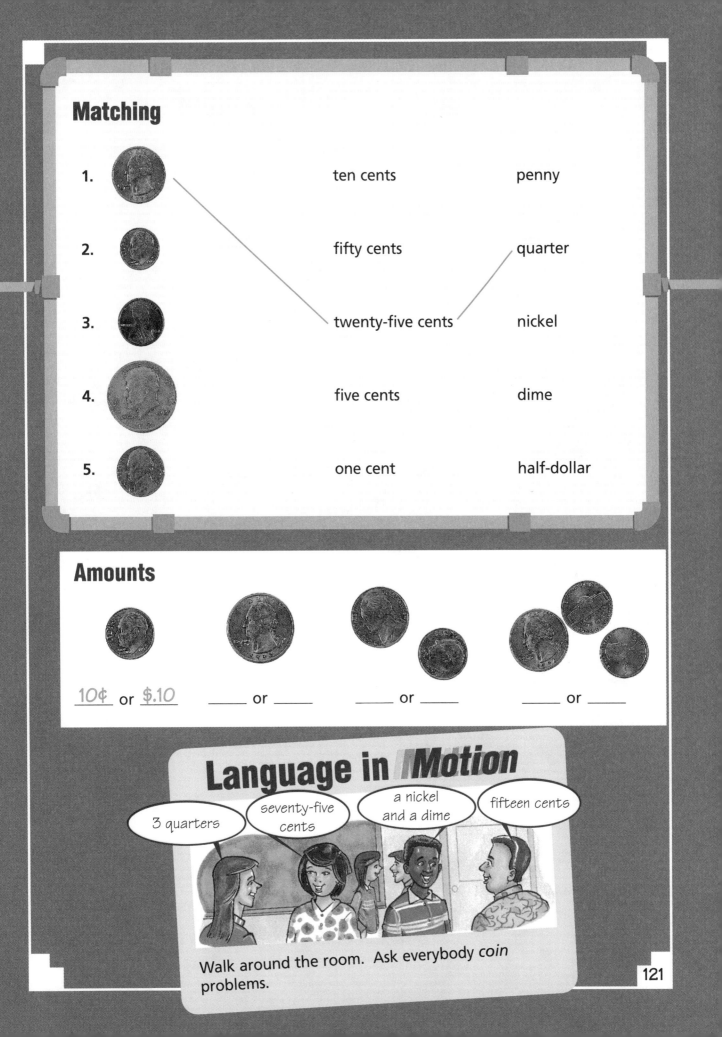

10¢ or $.10   ____ or ____   ____ or ____   ____ or ____

Language in Motion

3 quarters

seventy-five cents

a nickel and a dime

fifteen cents

Walk around the room. Ask everybody *coin* problems.

Bills

	a one-dollar bill **a dollar bill**	one dollar	$1.00
	a five-dollar bill	five dollars	$5.00
	a ten-dollar bill	ten dollars	$10.00
	a twenty-dollar bill	twenty dollars	$20.00
	a fifty-dollar bill	fifty dollars	$50.00
	a one hundred-dollar bill **a hundred-dollar bill**	one hundred dollars	$100.00

A. Look! I just found a ten-dollar bill!

B. Ten dollars! That's a lot of money!

Practice conversations with a partner. Use other bills.

A. Look! I just found a _____ bill!

B. _____ dollars! That's a lot of money!

Listening

Listen and write the number under the correct bills and coins.

_____

_____

_____

_____

1

_____

Listening

Listen and circle the correct amount.

1. $1.00	($5.00)	**5.** $.01	$1.00
2. $10.00	10¢	**6.** 75¢	$75.00
3. 25¢	$25.00	**7.** 5¢	$5.00
4. 50¢	25¢	**8.** $100.00	$10.00

Language in Motion

I just found a nickel.

I just found a nickel and a dime.

I just found a nickel, a dime, and a ten-dollar bill.

Stand in a circle. Repeat the money you hear. Add more money.

HOW MUCH DO I OWE YOU?

A. How much do I owe you?

B. Six dollars and fifty-five cents.

A. Six fifty-five?

B. Yes. That's right.

Practice conversations with a partner.

A. How much do I owe you?

B. _____.

A. _____?

B. Yes. That's right.

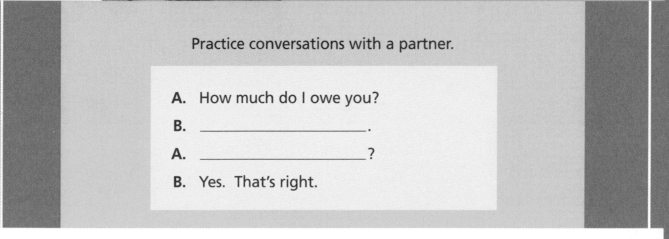

1.   2.   3.   4.   5.

Listening

Listen and circle the amount of money you hear.

1. ($9.95) $9.59   4. $16.45 $6.54

2. $88.10 $10.88   5. $14.50 $14.15

3. $44.79 $4.90   6. $20.02 $2.20

MAKING CHANGE

$17.50

$2.50

A. That's $17.50.

B. Here's $20.

A. Your change is $2.50.

Practice conversations with a partner.

A. That's _____.

B. Here's _____.

A. Your change is _____.

$8.75

$38.00

$3.55

1. $1.25

2. $2.00

3. $1.45

$48.50

$56.75

$96.10

4. $1.50

5. $3.25

6. $3.90

WHERE'S THE CHECKBOOK?

A. Where's the checkbook?
B. Here it is.

Practice conversations with a partner.

A. Where's the _____?
B. Here it is.

1. check

2. bank book

3. credit card

4. ATM card

5. deposit slip

6. withdrawal slip

Listening

Listen and write the number under the correct picture.

_____   _____   _____

_____   _____   1

These Are Things I Use

1. When I write a check, I use my   withdrawal slip.

2. When I put money in the bank, I use a   checkbook.

3. When I take money out of the bank, I use a   ATM card.

4. When I charge items in a store, I use my   deposit slip.

5. When I use a machine at the bank, I use my   credit card.

COMMUNITY ⊚ CONNECTIONS

Do you have a bank account? Where?
Do you have a checkbook? an ATM card? a credit card?
What banks do students in your class use?
Make a list of banks and their locations.

Bank	Location

I'M WRITING A CHECK

Fernando and Isabela Solano
56-98 Brookside Avenue, Apt 2-H
Freeport, RI 02915

226

January 9, 19 99

PAY TO THE ORDER OF *Wilson's Department Store* $ 95.50

Ninety-five dollars and 50/100 dollars

Muni Bank, NA
The Muni Bank
577 Park Road
Elmont, RI 02891

FOR _____ *Isabela Solano*

A. **What are you doing?**

B. **I'm writing a check to Wilson's Department Store.**

A. **For how much?**

B. **$95.50.**

Practice conversations with a partner.

A. **What are you doing?**

B. **I'm writing a check to _____.**

A. **For how much?**

B. **_____.**

Fernando and Isabela Solano
56-98 Brookside Avenue, Apt 2-H
Freeport, RI 02915

227

January 9, 19 99

PAY TO THE ORDER OF *Dr. Jackson* $ 60.00

Sixty and 00/100 dollars

Muni Bank, NA
The Muni Bank
577 Park Road
Elmont, RI 02891

FOR *check-up* *Isabela Solano*

1.

Fernando and Isabela Solano
56-98 Brookside Avenue, Apt 2-H
Freeport, RI 02915

228

January 9, 19 99

PAY TO THE ORDER OF *Ajax Cleaners* $ 29.95

Twenty-nine and 95/100 dollars

Muni Bank, NA
The Muni Bank
577 Park Road
Elmont, RI 02891

FOR *cleaning* *Isabela Solano*

2.

Fernando and Isabela Solano
56-98 Brookside Avenue, Apt 2-H
Freeport, RI 02915

229

January 9, 19 99

PAY TO THE ORDER OF *Davis Drug Store* $ 43.65

Forty-three and 65/100 dollars

Muni Bank, NA
The Muni Bank
577 Park Road
Elmont, RI 02891

FOR *medicine* *Isabela Solano*

3.

Fernando and Isabela Solano
56-98 Brookside Avenue, Apt 2-H
Freeport, RI 02915

230

January 9, 19 99

PAY TO THE ORDER OF *Westville Hospital* $ 250.00

Two hundred fifty and 00/100 dollars

Muni Bank, NA
The Muni Bank
577 Park Road
Elmont, RI 02891

FOR *blood tests* *Isabela Solano*

4.

Writing Checks

Write the dollar amounts and sign your name.

1. $17.25

	250
	1-2/10 Branch 440

January 9 19 *99*

PAY TO THE ORDER OF *Howard Cleaner's* $ *17.50*

Seventeen and 50/100 _____ dollars

Muni Bank, NA
The Muni Bank
577 Park Road
Elmont, RI 02891

FOR *cleaning*

0210000021 440 507431 0250

2. $50.00

	251
	1-2/10 Branch 440

January 9 19 *99*

PAY TO THE ORDER OF *Dr. Brown* $ *50.00*

_____ dollars

Muni Bank, NA
The Muni Bank
577 Park Road
Elmont, RI 02891

FOR *office visit*

0210000021 440 507431 0251

3. $67.75

	252
	1-2/10 Branch 440

January 9 19 *99*

PAY TO THE ORDER OF *Arnold's Drug Store* $ *67.75*

_____ dollars

Muni Bank, NA
The Muni Bank
577 Park Road
Elmont, RI 02891

FOR *prescriptions*

0210000021 440 507431 0252

4. $119.90

	253
	1-2/10 Branch 440

January 9 19 *99*

PAY TO THE ORDER OF *International Express* $ *119.90*

_____ dollars

Muni Bank, NA
The Muni Bank
577 Park Road
Elmont, RI 02891

FOR *monthly bill*

0210000021 440 507431 0253

COMMUNITY ⊙ CONNECTIONS

How much do you pay for the following?

a loaf of bread _____

a quart of milk _____

a gallon of gas _____

a movie _____

rent _____

electricity _____

DIFFERENT CULTURES   DIFFERENT WAYS

Different countries have different coins and bills.

What are the names of coins and bills in *your* country? What are their values? What coins and bills from other countries do you know?

In your country, how much do you pay for the items in Community Connections above?

Language Experience Journal

Saving Money

In your Language Experience Journal, write about ways you save money. Do you buy things on sale? Do you shop at discount stores? Do you go to yard sales? Or, tell your ideas so your teacher can write them. Then read your suggestions to a classmate.

PUT IT TOGETHER — PART A

INFORMATION GAP ACTIVITY

Work with a partner. You each have prices for different items in the same fast-food restaurant. Ask each other questions to find out the prices of all the items.

a hamburger	$1.60
a cheeseburger	$1.75
a taco	_____
a pizza	$3.50
a sandwich	$2.25
coffee	_____
tea	$.75
milk	_____

How much is a hamburger?

A hamburger is $1.60.

INFORMATION GAP ACTIVITY

Work with a partner. You each have prices for different items in the same fast-food restaurant. Ask each other questions to find out the prices of all the items.

a hamburger	$1.60
a cheeseburger	_____
a taco	$1.35
a pizza	_____
a sandwich	_____
coffee	$.75
tea	_____
milk	$.80

How much is a hamburger?

A hamburger is $1.60.

Vocabulary Foundations

penny
nickel
dime
quarter
half-dollar
one-dollar bill
five-dollar bill
ten-dollar bill
twenty-dollar bill
fifty-dollar bill
one-hundred dollar bill
check
checkbook
bank book
credit card
ATM card
deposit slip
withdrawal slip

Language Skill Foundations

I can . . .

☐ identify coins and bills

☐ tell the value of coins and bills

☐ write amounts of coins and bills

☐ purchase items in a store

☐ make change when purchasing an item

☐ identify basic banking items

☐ describe basic banking procedures

☐ write checks

☐ compare the cost of everyday items

☐ identify coins and bills from different countries

☐ tell ways to save money

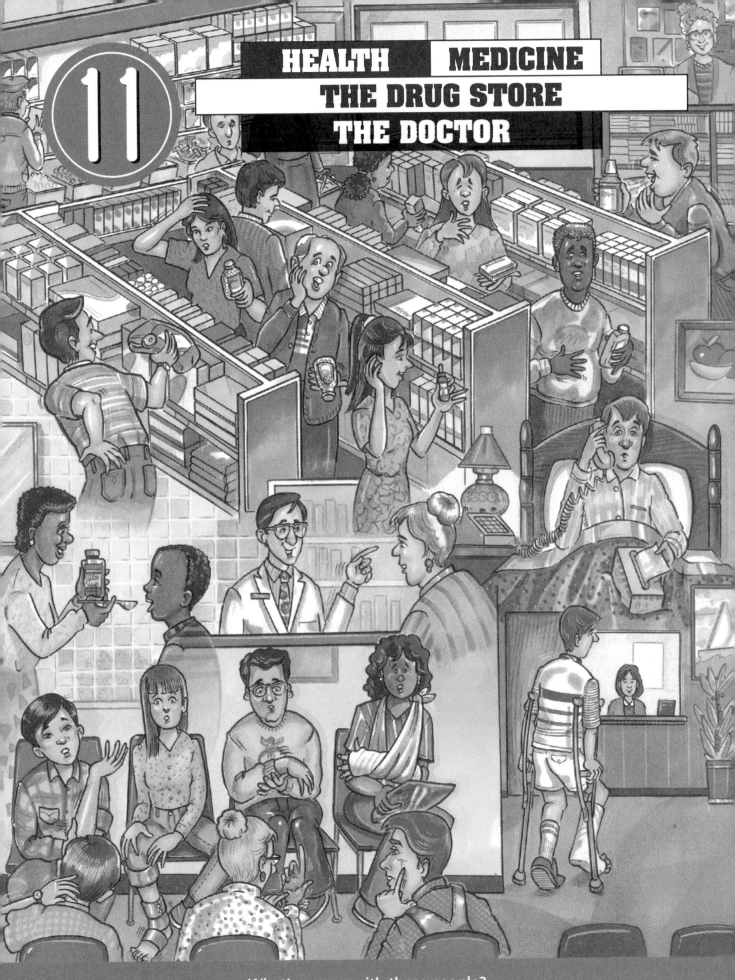

11

HEALTH MEDICINE
THE DRUG STORE
THE DOCTOR

What's wrong with these people?
What are they saying?

AILMENTS

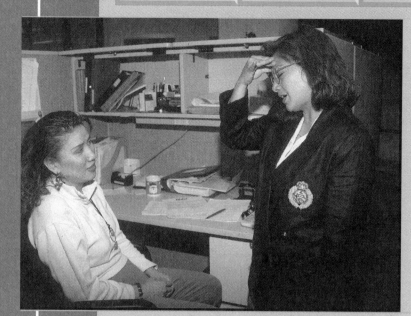

A. What's the matter?

B. I have a headache.

Practice conversations with a partner.

A. What's the matter?

B. I have _____.

1. a stomachache

2. a backache

3. a toothache

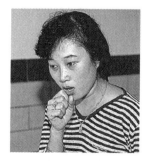

4. an earache

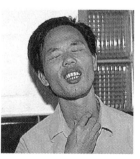

5. a sore throat

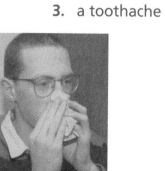

6. a cold

7. a cough

Construction Site

I	have	
You	have	a headache.
He	has	
She	has	

1. He ___has___ a headache.

2. I _____ an earache.

3. She _____ a toothache.

4. You _____ a sore throat.

5. I _____ a stomachache.

6. He _____ a cold.

Listening

Listen and write the number under the correct picture.

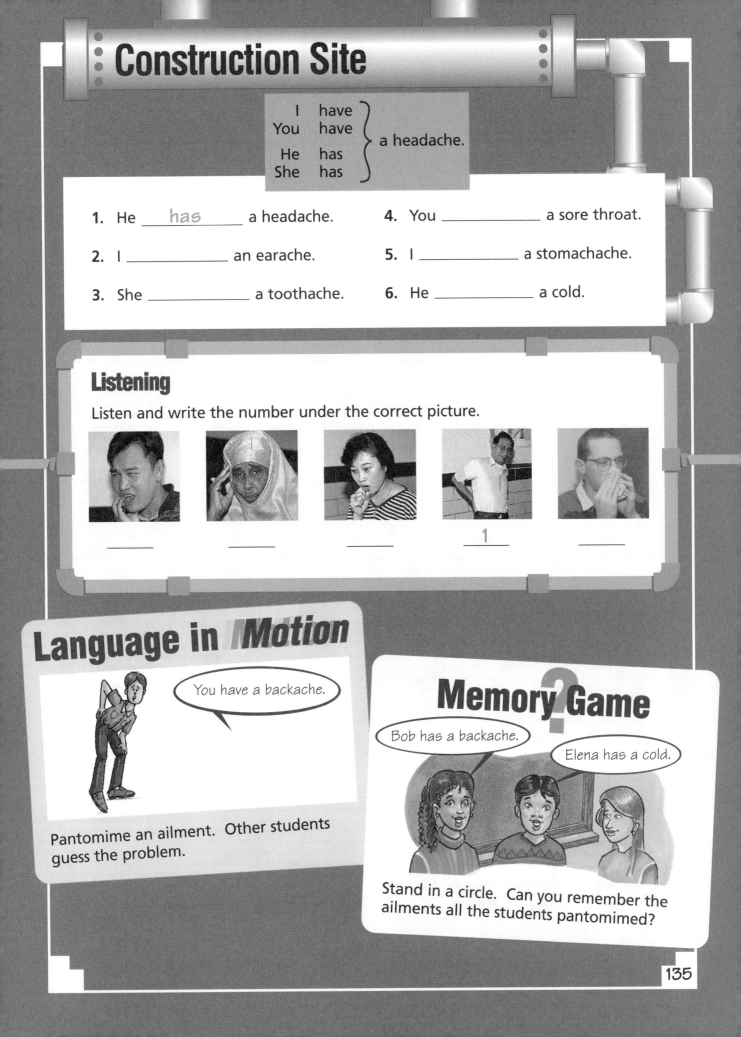

_____   _____   _____   __1__   _____

Language in Motion

You have a backache.

Pantomime an ailment. Other students guess the problem.

Memory Game

Bob has a backache.

Elena has a cold.

Stand in a circle. Can you remember the ailments all the students pantomimed?

MEDICINE

A. I have a cough. What should I do?
B. You should use cough syrup.

Practice conversations with a partner.

A. I have _____. What should I do?
B. You should use _____.

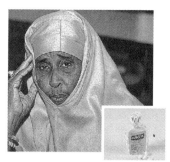

1. aspirin

2. ear drops

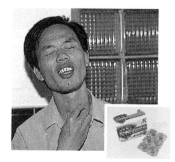

3. throat lozenges

4. cold medicine

5. antacid tablets

Listening

Listen and put a check under the correct medicine.

1. _____ ✓ _____

2. _____ _____

3. _____ _____

4. _____ _____

5. _____ _____

6. _____ _____

Matching

1. When I have a cold, I use   antacid tablets.

2. When I have an earache, I use   cough syrup.

3. When I have a sore throat, I use   cold medicine.

4. When I have a stomachache, I use   ear drops.

5. When I have a cough, I use   throat lozenges.

Listening

Listen and circle the ailment.

1. (sore throat)   headache   4. stomachache   headache

2. stomachache   earache   5. earache   stomachache

3. cold   stomachache   6. cough   headache

WHERE CAN I FIND COUGH SYRUP?

A. Excuse me. Where can I find cough syrup?

B. Look in Aisle 1.

A. Thank you.

Practice conversations with a partner. Use the drug store diagram above.

A. Excuse me. Where can I find _____?

B. Look in _____.

A. Thank you.

TAKING MEDICINE

A. **Here's your medicine. Take one pill three times a day.**

B. **I understand. One pill three times a day.**

A. **That's right.**

Practice conversations with a partner.

A. Here's your medicine. Take _____.

B. I understand. _____.

A. That's right.

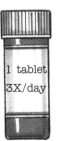

1. one tablet
three times a day

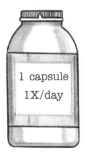

2. one capsule
once a day

3. one teaspoon
before each meal

4. two teaspoons
after each meal

Matching

1. Take one pill three times a day.

2. Take two tablets once a day.

3. Take three capsules twice a day.

4. Take one teaspoon before each meal.

5. Take two tablets after each meal.

Listening

Listen and circle.

1.	2 pills	(1 pill)	5.	2X/day	3X/day
2.	1 teaspoon	2 teaspoons	6.	4X/day	2X/day
3.	2 capsules	2 pills	7.	before	after
4.	1 tablet	1 teaspoon	8.	before	after

Missing Letters

1. c a p s u l e
2. _ _ b _ e _
3. _ e _ s _ _ o _

4. _ e _ i c _ _ e
5. _ i _ _
6. _ _ s l e

COMMUNITY CONNECTIONS

Visit a local drug store. Ask the pharmacist to recommend medicine for different ailments. Write down the brand names. Compare information with other students.

My Pharmacist's Recommendations

For a headache: _____

For a stomachache: _____

For a sore throat: _____

For a backache: _____

For a cold: _____

For a cough: _____

For an earache: _____

DIFFERENT CULTURES　DIFFERENT WAYS

Different cultures have different remedies for common medical problems.

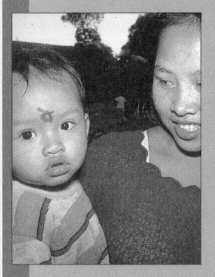

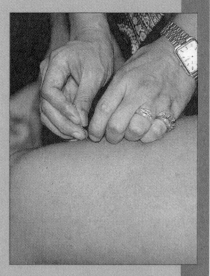

What remedies do you see?
What medical problems are they for?

What are some remedies for medical problems in your culture?

Language Experience Journal

When I'm Sick

What do you do when you have a cold? a stomachache? a sore throat? a toothache? In your Language Experience Journal, write about the things you do when you're sick. Or, tell your ideas so your teacher can write them. Then read about your medical treatments to a classmate.

I feel dizzy.

My neck is stiff.

My arm is swollen.

My back hurts.

My shoulder hurts.

I twisted my ankle.

I broke my arm.

I broke my leg.

I sprained my wrist.

I cut my finger.

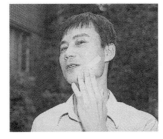

I cut my face.

I burned my hand.

CALLING THE DOCTOR

A. Doctor's office.

B. Hello. This is Peter Chen. I want to make an appointment.

A. What's the problem?

B. I have a bad stomachache.

A. Can you come in tomorrow at 2:15?

B. Yes. That's fine.

Practice conversations with another student. Use your own name
and any ailments, injuries, and times you wish.

A. Doctor's office.

B. Hello. This is _____. I want to make an
appointment.

A. What's the problem?

B. _____.

A. Can you come in _____ at _____?

B. Yes. That's fine.

Listening

Listen and write the number under the correct picture.

_____

_____

1

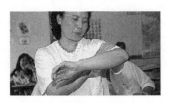

_____

_____

_____

_____

_____

_____

PUT IT TOGETHER

PART A

INFORMATION GAP ACTIVITY

Work with a partner. You each have different information about the same drug store. Ask each other questions to find the medicines.

aspirin	Aisle 4
throat lozenges	**Aisle 3**
ear drops	**Aisle 7**
cold medicine	_____
cough syrup	**Aisle 9**
antacid tablets	_____

Where can I find aspirin?

Look in Aisle 4.

Work with a partner. You each have different information about the same drug store. Ask each other questions to find the medicines.

> Where can I find aspirin?

> Look in Aisle 4.

aspirin	**Aisle 4**
throat lozenges	_____
ear drops	_____
cold medicine	**Aisle 6**
cough syrup	_____
antacid tablets	**Aisle 11**

Vocabulary Foundations

backache	ankle
earache	arm
headache	back
stomachache	face
toothache	finger
cold	hand
cough	leg
sore throat	neck
antacid tablets	shoulder
aspirin	wrist
cold medicine	broke
cough syrup	burned
ear drops	cut
throat lozenges	dizzy
aisle	sprained
capsule	stiff
pill	swollen
tablet	twisted
teaspoon	

Language Skill Foundations

I can . . .

☐ name common ailments

☐ name common medicines

☐ identify treatments for common ailments

☐ locate medicine in a drug store

☐ identify dosages on a medicine label

☐ ask a pharmacist for advice about medicine

☐ compare medical treatments in different cultures

☐ identify common medical problems and injuries

☐ call a doctor's office to schedule an appointment

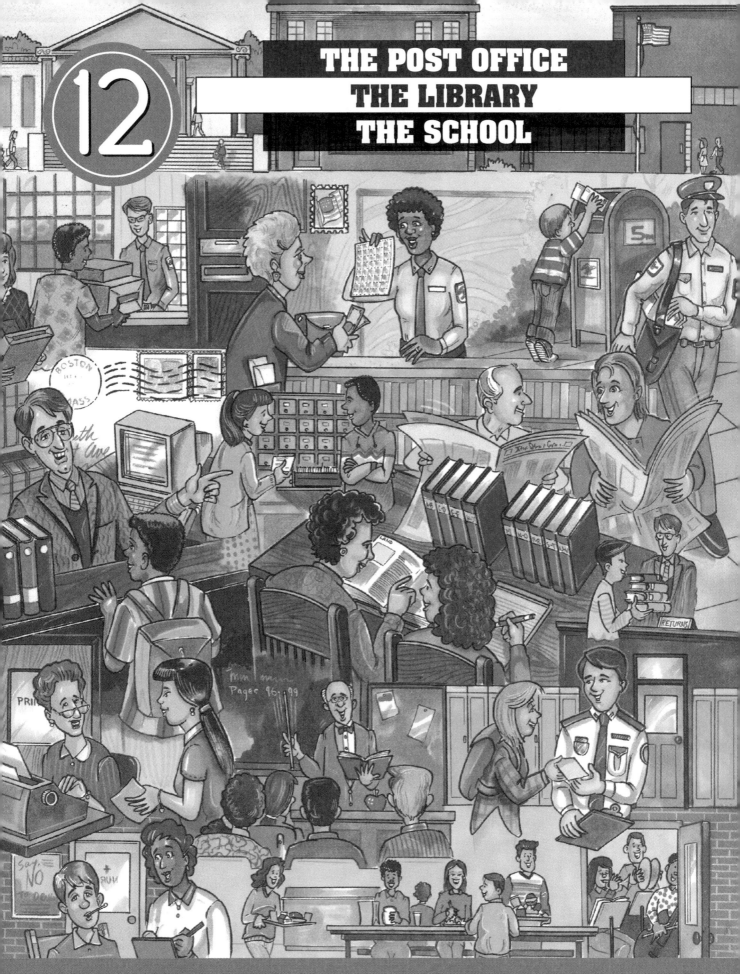

12

THE POST OFFICE
THE LIBRARY
THE SCHOOL

What places do you see?
What are people doing?

AT THE POST OFFICE

A. **I want to buy stamps.**

B. **You can buy stamps at the next window.**

A. **Thank you.**

Practice conversations with a partner.

A. I want to _____.

B. You can _____ at the next window.

A. Thank you.

1. mail a package

2. buy a money order

3. send a registered letter

4. buy an aerogramme

Matching

Look at the pictures and draw a line.

1 STAMPS	2 MONEY ORDERS	3 REGISTERED MAIL	4 PACKAGES	5 AEROGRAMMES

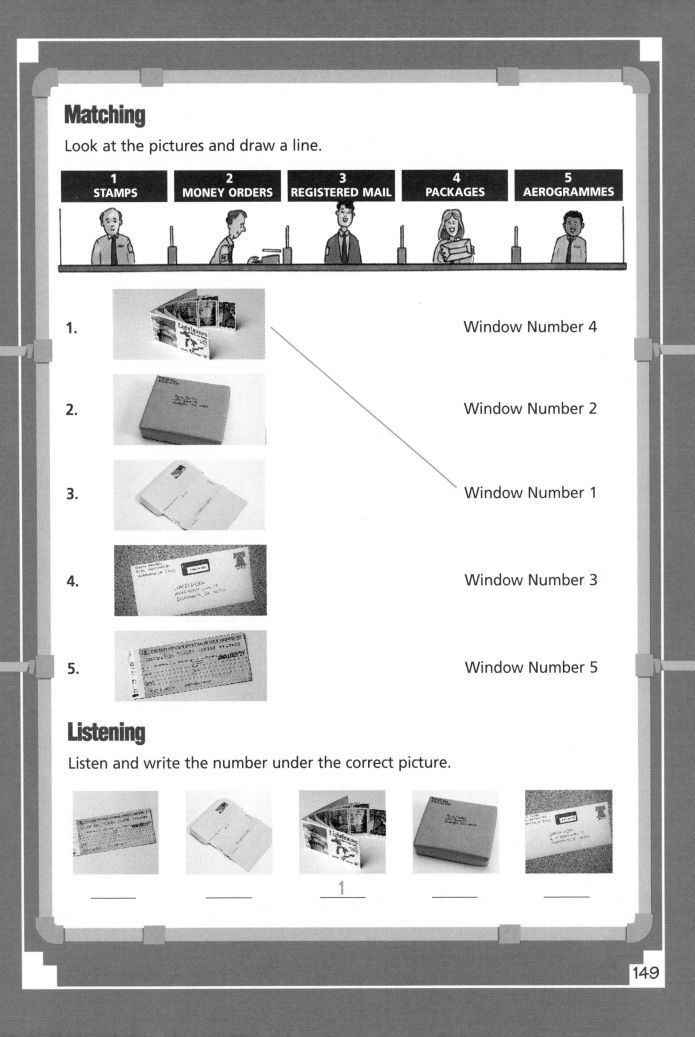

1.   Window Number 4

2.   Window Number 2

3.   Window Number 1

4.   Window Number 3

5.   Window Number 5

Listening

Listen and write the number under the correct picture.

___   ___   _1_   ___   ___

An Envelope

Henry Wong
1415 Center Street
Boston, MA 02218

Roberta Fernandez
977 Westwood Avenue
Los Angeles, CA 90024

1. Who is this letter going to? _____

2. What's the return address? _____

COMMUNITY CONNECTIONS

Go to your local post office. Find out the following information:

What days is the post office open? _____

When does the post office open? _____

When does it close? _____

Language Experience Journal

The Foundations Letter Exchange

Write a letter to a classmate. Write about anything you want. Or, say your letter so your teacher can write it. Mail your letter. Answer the letter you receive from a different classmate.

AT THE LIBRARY

A. Excuse me. Where's the card catalog?

B. Over there.

A. Thanks.

A. Excuse me. Where are the magazines?

B. Over there.

A. Thanks.

Practice conversations with a partner.

1. checkout desk

2. books

3. dictionaries

4. librarian

5. tapes

6. encyclopedias

Listening

Listen and write the number under the correct picture.

_____   _____   ____1____   _____

_____   _____   _____   _____

COMMUNITY CONNECTIONS

Visit your local library. Find out the following information:

What days is the library open? _____

When does the library open? _____

When does it close? _____

For how long can you borrow a
    book? _____

Where are the dictionaries and
    encyclopedias? _____

How many books are there
    in the library? _____

Does the library have books in your
    first language? What kind? _____

PEOPLE AT SCHOOL

A. **Who's that?**

B. **That's the E.S.L. teacher.**

Practice conversations with a partner.

A. Who's that?

B. That's the _____.

1. principal

2. school nurse

3. guidance counselor

4. P.E. teacher

5. custodian

PLACES AT SCHOOL

A. **Where are you going?**

B. **To the office.**

Practice conversations with a partner.

A. Where are you going?

B. To the _____.

1. principal's office

2. guidance office

3. nurse's office

4. cafeteria

5. auditorium

6. gym

Listening

Listen and put a check under the correct picture.

1. _____ __✓___

2. _____ _____

3. _____ _____

4. _____ _____

5. _____ _____

6. _____ _____

7. _____ _____

8. _____ _____

Missing Letters

1. o f f i c e

2. _ _ m

3. _ r i _ _ i _ a _

4. _ _ r s e

5. _ _ d _ t _ r _ _ _

6. _ a _ e _ _ r _ a

SCHOOL SUBJECTS

A. **What's your favorite subject?**

B. **Math.**

Practice conversations with a partner.

A. What's your favorite subject?

B. _____.

1. English

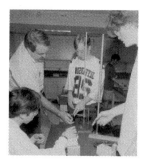

2. science

3. history

4. technology

5. art

6. music

Listening

Listen and write the number under the correct picture.

_____   1   _____

_____   _____   _____

Unscramble the Subjects

1. hmat   _____math_____   4. gEhisln   _____
2. rta   _____   5. thoyisr   _____
3. nicesec   _____   6. smuci   _____

Language in Motion

What's your favorite subject?

Walk around the room. Ask all the students about their favorite school subjects.

Memory Game

Maria's favorite subject is science.

Tom's favorite subject is art.

Stand in a circle. Can you remember everybody's favorite subject?

EXTRACURRICULAR ACTIVITIES

A. What are you going to do after school today?

B. I have band practice.

Practice conversations with a partner.

A. What are you going to do after school today?

B. I have _____ practice.

1. orchestra

2. choir

3. drama

4. football

Schools in different countries around the world can be very different.

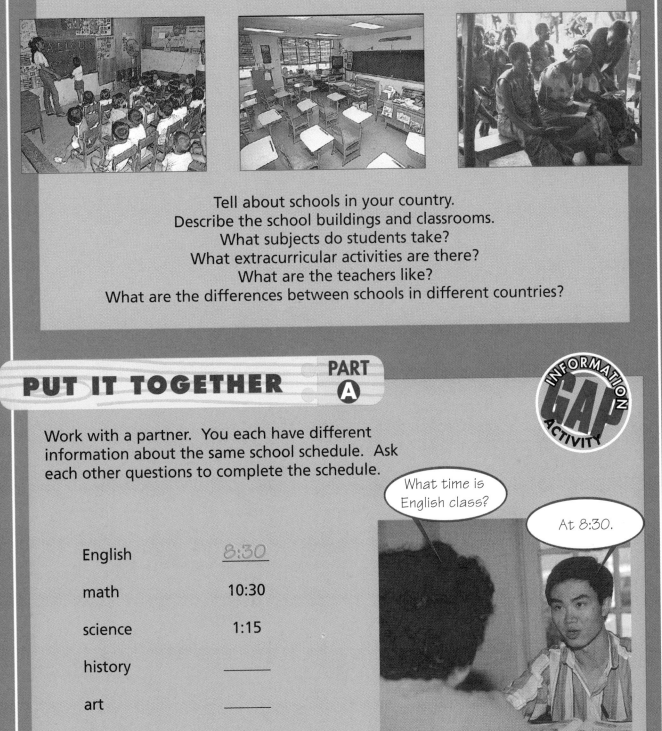

Tell about schools in your country.
Describe the school buildings and classrooms.
What subjects do students take?
What extracurricular activities are there?
What are the teachers like?
What are the differences between schools in different countries?

PUT IT TOGETHER   PART A

INFORMATION GAP ACTIVITY

Work with a partner. You each have different information about the same school schedule. Ask each other questions to complete the schedule.

What time is English class?

At 8:30.

English   8:30

math   10:30

science   1:15

history   _____

art   _____

music   _____

technology   2:45

Work with a partner. You each have different information about the same school schedule. Ask each other questions to complete the schedule.

What time is English class?

At 8:30.

English	8:30
math	_____
science	_____
history	9:30
art	11:30
music	2:00
technology	_____

Vocabulary Foundations

aerogramme
money order
package
registered letter
return address
stamp
buy
mail
send
books
card catalog
checkout desk
dictionaries
encyclopedias
librarian
magazines
tapes
custodian
guidance counselor
P.E. teacher

principal
school nurse
auditorium
cafeteria
guidance office
nurse's office
office
principal's office
art
band
choir
drama
English
football
gym
history
math
music
orchestra
science
technology

Language Skill Foundations

I can . . .

☐ name post office items

☐ obtain basic post office services

☐ find out my local post office's hours

☐ name library items

☐ find out information about my local library

☐ name school personnel

☐ name places in a school

☐ name school subjects

☐ name extracurricular activities

☐ compare schools in different countries

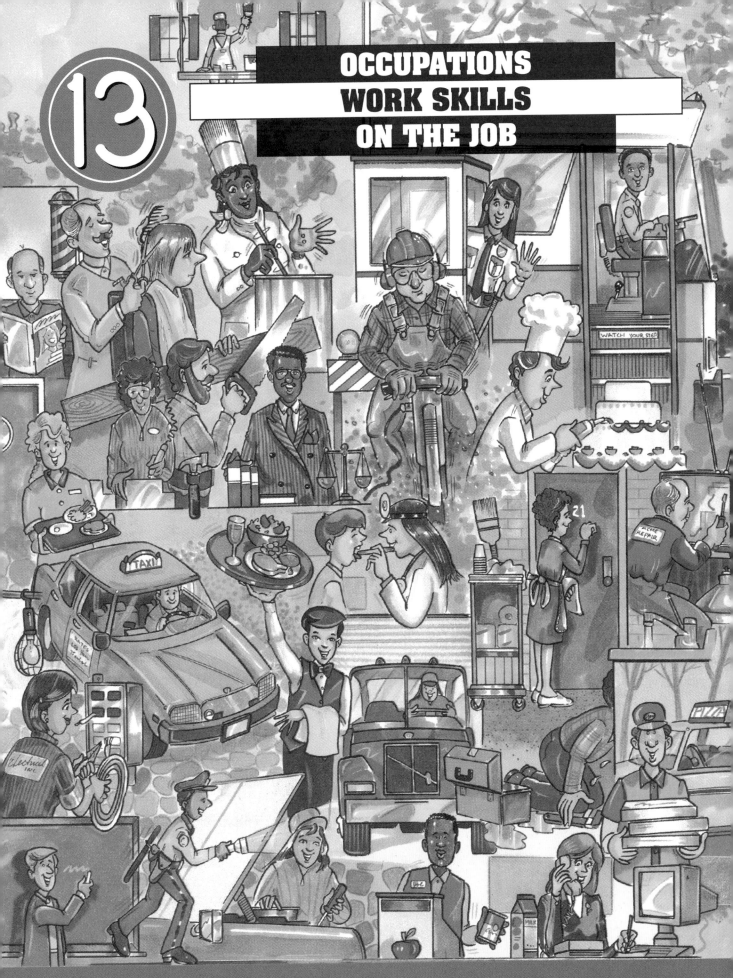

13

OCCUPATIONS
WORK SKILLS
ON THE JOB

What occupations do you see?

OCCUPATIONS

A. **What do you do?**

B. **I'm a barber.**

Practice conversations with a partner.

A. What do you do?

B. I'm _____.

1. a cook

2. a cashier

3. a delivery person

4. a security guard

5. an electrician

6. a repairperson

7. a police officer

8. a lawyer

9. a construction worker

Listening

Listen and write the number under the correct picture.

_____ _____ _____

_____ __1__ _____

Associations

1. cook   money
2. barber   building
3. security guard   food
4. cashier   truck
5. delivery person   hair

Missing Letters

1. l̲ a̲ w y̶ er   4. _ _ _ k
2. _ a _ _ i _ r   5. _ a _ _ e _
3. _ _ e _ t _ _ c _ a _   6. r _ _ _ _ r p _ _ _ o _

A. Can you drive a bus?

B. Yes, I can. I'm an experienced bus driver.

Practice conversations with a partner.

A. Can you _____?

B. Yes, I can. I'm an experienced _____.

1. bake
baker

2. type
secretary

3. fix cars
mechanic

4. drive a truck
truck driver

5. teach
teacher

6. paint
painter

7. fix sinks
plumber

8. drive a taxi
taxi driver

9. repair buildings
carpenter

Listening

Listen and put a check under the correct occupation.

1.
   _____   ✓_____

2.
   _____   _____

3.
   _____   _____

4.
   _____   _____

5. _____   _____

6.
   _____   _____

Language in Motion

You're a waiter!

You're a bus driver!

Pantomime an occupation. Other students guess what it is.

Matching

1. I'm a truck driver. I can
2. I'm a mechanic. I can
3. I'm a plumber. I can
4. I'm a secretary. I can
5. I'm a painter. I can
6. I'm a teacher. I can
7. I'm a bus driver. I can
8. I'm a carpenter. I can

fix sinks.

fix cars.

drive a truck.

drive a bus.

repair buildings.

paint.

type.

teach.

Language in Motion

Walk around the room. Ask all the students about their work skills.

Memory Game

Stand in a circle. Can you remember everybody's work skills?

Language Experience Journal

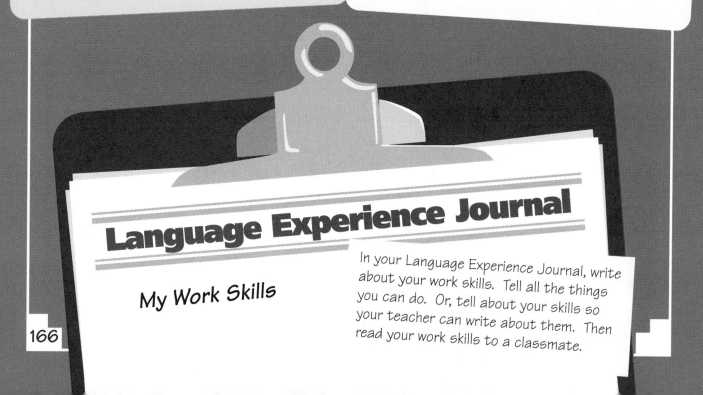

My Work Skills

In your Language Experience Journal, write about your work skills. Tell all the things you can do. Or, tell about your skills so your teacher can write about them. Then read your work skills to a classmate.

A. **What's your occupation?**

B. **I'm a waiter.**

A. **Where do you work?**

B. **At Waldo's Restaurant.**

Practice conversations with a partner.

A. What's your occupation?

B. I'm _____.

A. Where do you work?

B. At _____.

1. a waitress
the Greenhouse Cafe

2. a housekeeper
the Royal Hotel

3. an assembler
Ajax Electronics

4. a pharmacist
Federal Pharmacy

5. a salesperson
Blaine's Department Store

6. a doctor
Memorial Hospital

Matching

1. doctor   department store
2. waitress   hotel
3. salesperson   hospital
4. pharmacist   factory
5. housekeeper   restaurant
6. assembler   drug store

Listening

Listen and write the number under the place where these people work.

Language Experience Journal

Workplaces

Where do you work? Where do the people in your family work? Write about it in your Language Experience Journal. Or, tell about it so your teacher can write it. Then read your story to a classmate.

MORE WORK SKILLS

A. **Can you assemble components?**

B. **No, I can't. But I'm sure I can learn quickly.**

Practice conversations with a partner.

A. Can you _____?

B. No, I can't. But I'm sure I can learn quickly.

1. cook

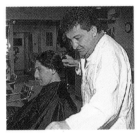

2. cut hair

3. sell clothing

4. operate equipment

5. repair watches

6. use a cash register

Listening

Listen and write the number under the correct picture.

_____

_____

_____

_____

__1__

_____

Finish the Sentence

1. An assembler ——————————— sells things in a store.

2. A barber ———————————————— assembles components.

3. A cook   repairs things.

4. A salesperson   cuts hair.

5. A repairperson   cooks food in a restaurant.

Can You ...?

Answer these questions about your work skills.

	Yes, I can.	No, I can't.
1. Can you assemble things?	_____	_____
2. Can you repair things?	_____	_____
3. Can you operate equipment?	_____	_____
4. Can you use a cash register?	_____	_____

LOCATIONS

A. **Excuse me. Where's the cafeteria?**

B. **Down the hall.**

A. **Thanks.**

Practice conversations with a partner.

A. **Excuse me. Where's the _____?**

B. **Down the hall.**

A. **Thanks.**

1. supply room

2. Personnel Office

3. employee lounge

4. mailroom

5. bathroom

6. vending machine

171

Listening

Listen and write the number under the correct picture.

_____   _____   __1__

_____   _____   _____

What's the Answer?

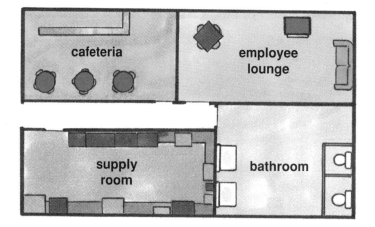

1. It's across from the cafeteria.   _supply room_

2. It's next to the supply room.   _____

3. It's next to the cafeteria.   _____

SAFETY AT WORK

A. **Careful!**

B. **Excuse me?**

A. **The floor is wet!**

B. **Okay. Thanks for telling me.**

Practice conversations with a partner.

A. Careful!

B. Excuse me?

A. _____!

B. Okay. Thanks for telling me.

1.

2.

3.

4.

Listening

Listen and write the number under the correct picture.

_____

_____

___1___

_____

COMMUNITY CONNECTIONS

Visit three workplaces in your community. What jobs do you see?

Workplace	Jobs
1. _____	_____
2. _____	_____
3. _____	_____

174

Men and women sometimes have different jobs in different cultures.

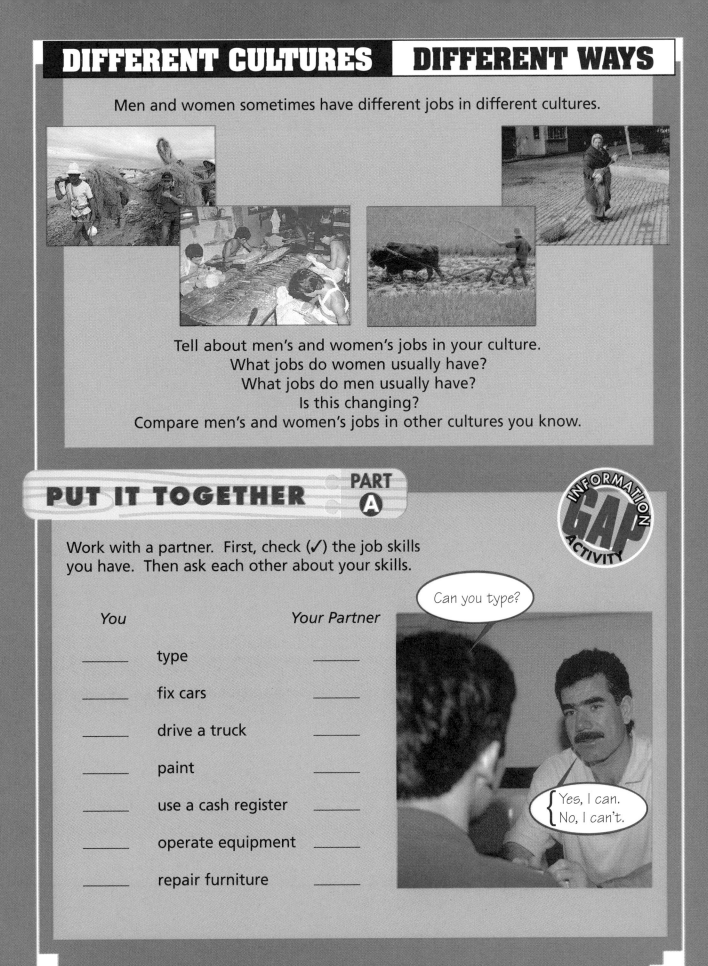

Tell about men's and women's jobs in your culture.
What jobs do women usually have?
What jobs do men usually have?
Is this changing?
Compare men's and women's jobs in other cultures you know.

PUT IT TOGETHER   PART A

INFORMATION GAP ACTIVITY

Work with a partner. First, check (✓) the job skills you have. Then ask each other about your skills.

Can you type?

Yes, I can.
No, I can't.

You		Your Partner
_____	type	_____
_____	fix cars	_____
_____	drive a truck	_____
_____	paint	_____
_____	use a cash register	_____
_____	operate equipment	_____
_____	repair furniture	_____

Work with a partner. First, check (✓) the job skills you have. Then ask each other about your skills.

You		Your Partner
_____	type	_____
_____	fix cars	_____
_____	drive a truck	_____
_____	paint	_____
_____	use a cash register	_____
_____	operate equipment	_____
_____	repair furniture	_____

Can you type?

Yes, I can.
No, I can't.

Vocabulary Foundations

assembler
baker
barber
bus driver
carpenter
cashier
construction worker
cook
delivery person
doctor
electrician
housekeeper
lawyer
mechanic
painter
pharmacist
plumber
police officer

repairperson
salesperson
secretary
security guard
taxi driver
teacher
truck driver
waiter
waitress
assemble
bake
cook
cut
drive
fix
operate
paint
repair
sell

teach
type
use
employee lounge
mailroom
Personnel Office
supply room
vending machine

Language Skill Foundations

I can . . .

☐ name occupations

☐ describe my work skills

☐ name work sites

☐ express confidence during a job interview

☐ locate places and facilities at work

☐ give and understand safety warnings

☐ ask for repetition

☐ compare men's and women's jobs in different cultures

DIRECTIONS
PUBLIC TRANSPORTATION

What do you see?
What are people saying?

ASKING DIRECTIONS

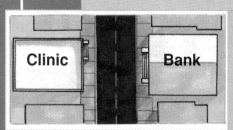

Clinic   Bank

Library

A. Excuse me. How do I get to the *bank?*

B. Walk that way. The *bank* is on the *right, across from the clinic.*

A. Excuse me. How do I get to the *library?*

B. Walk that way. The *library* is on the *left, next to the park.*

Practice conversations with a partner.

A. Excuse me. How do I get to the _____?

B. Walk that way. The _____ is on the right/left, across from/next to the _____.

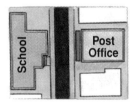

1. laundromat

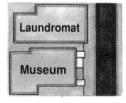

2. post office

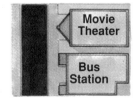

3. movie theater

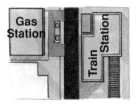

4. gas station

5. drug store

6. shopping mall

178

Left or Right?

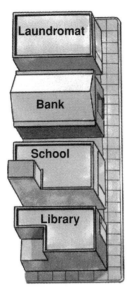

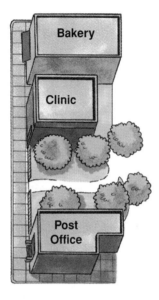

1. The laundromat is on the ___left___.
2. The park is on the _____.
3. The school is on the _____.
4. The bakery is on the _____.

5. The post office is on the _____.
6. The library is on the _____.
7. The bank is on the _____.
8. The clinic is on the _____.

Listening

Look at the street scene above. Listen and circle the correct place.

1. (laundromat)   clinic
2. clinic   school
3. post office   park
4. school   clinic

5. bank   library
6. bakery   park
7. library   school
8. bakery   bank

Language in Motion

Work with some classmates. Write the names of buildings on cards. Stand up, hold the cards, and be a street! Other students should then ask and give directions to the buildings on your "street".

Memory Game

Can you remember the locations in the activity above? Stand in a circle. Give a location and see if the person next to you agrees.

A. **Which bus goes to Midvale?**

B. **Bus Number 9.**

A. **Bus Number 9?**

B. **Yes. That's right.**

Practice conversations with a partner.

A. Which _____ goes _____?

B. _____.

A. _____?

B. Yes. That's right.

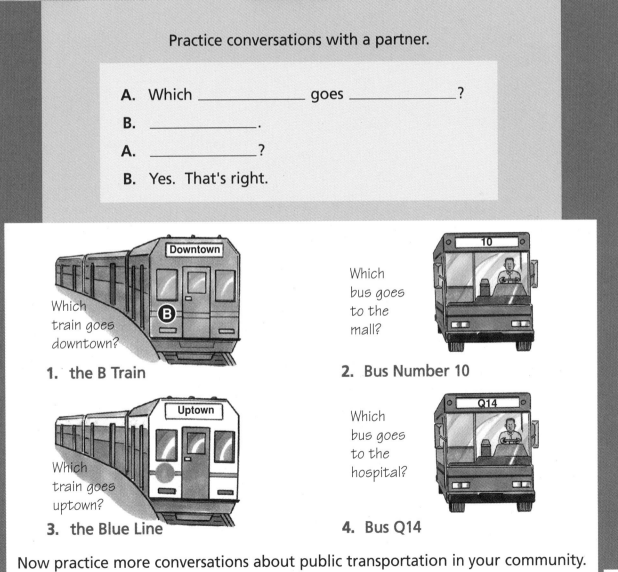

Which train goes downtown?

1. the B Train

Which bus goes to the mall?

2. Bus Number 10

Which train goes uptown?

3. the Blue Line

Which bus goes to the hospital?

4. Bus Q14

Now practice more conversations about public transportation in your community.

Matching

1. Riverside   Bus Number 64

2. Easton   the C Train

3. Riverdale   the Blue Line

4. Weston   the Number 19 bus

Listening

Listen and put a check under the correct picture.

1. _____   ✓_____   **2.** _____   _____

3. _____   _____   **4.** _____   _____

5. _____   _____   **6.** _____   _____

USING PUBLIC TRANSPORTATION

A. Excuse me. How do I get to City Hospital?

B. Take the C Train and get off at Rice Road.

A. Thanks very much.

Practice conversations with a partner.

A. Excuse me. How do I get to _____?

B. Take _____ and get off at _____.

A. Thanks very much.

1. the zoo
   Bus Number 11

2. Blake's Department Store
   the Yellow line

3. the airport
   the F Train

4. the Lakeside Mall
   Bus Number 7

Now practice more conversations about public transportation in your community.

Listening

Listen and put a check next to the correct picture.

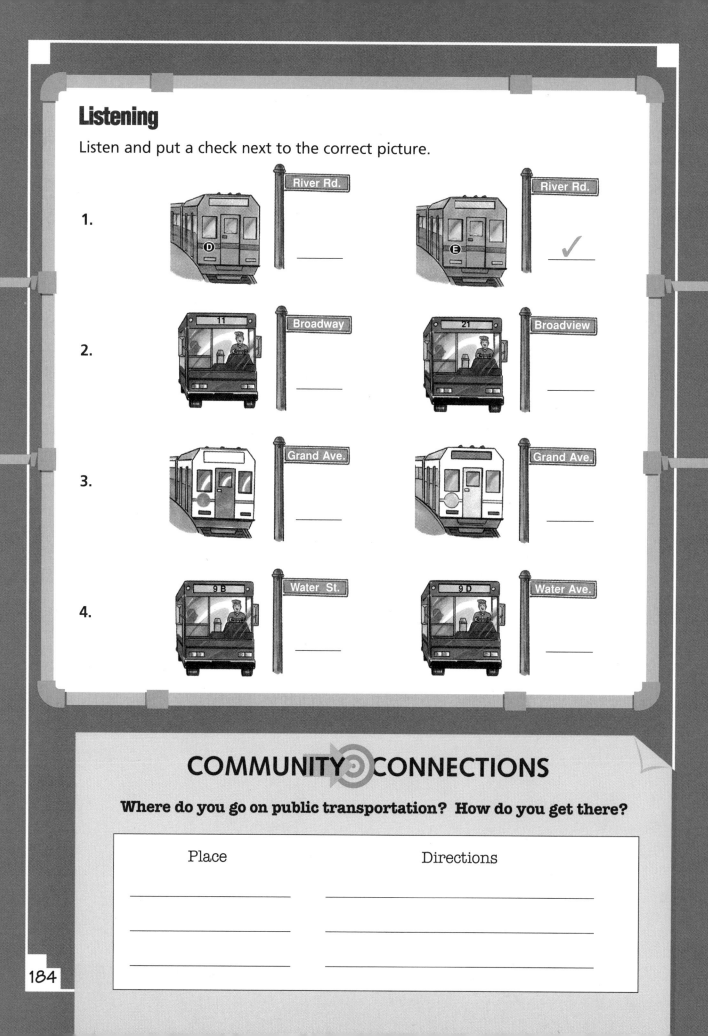

1.

2.

3.

4.

COMMUNITY CONNECTIONS

Where do you go on public transportation? How do you get there?

Place	Directions

DRIVING PLACES

Drive to River Street and turn right.

A. Can you tell me how to get to the Westside Mall?

B. Drive to River Street and turn right.

A. Thanks.

Practice conversations with a partner.

A. Can you tell me how to get to _____?

B. _____.

A. Thanks.

Drive to Grove Street and turn left.

1. the Midtown Movie Theater

Take the interstate and get off at Exit 9.

2. Dave's Discount Store

Take the expressway and get off at Green Street.

3. the Science Museum

Go over the Bay Bridge and get off at Exit 3.

4. the airport

Now practice more conversations about locations in your community.

Matching

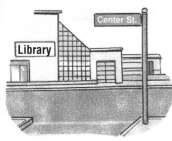

1. Can you tell me how to get to the Bayside Mall?

   Drive to Center Street and turn right.

2. Can you tell me how to get to the zoo?

   Take the interstate and get off at Tyler Road.

3. Can you tell me how to get to the museum?

   Drive to Center Street and turn left.

4. Can you tell me how to get to the library?

   Go over the Tower Bridge and take Exit 1.

5. Can you tell me how to get to the hospital?

   Take the expressway and get off at Exit 9.

COMMUNITY CONNECTIONS

What are some places you drive to? How do you get there?

Place	Directions

DEPARTURE TIMES

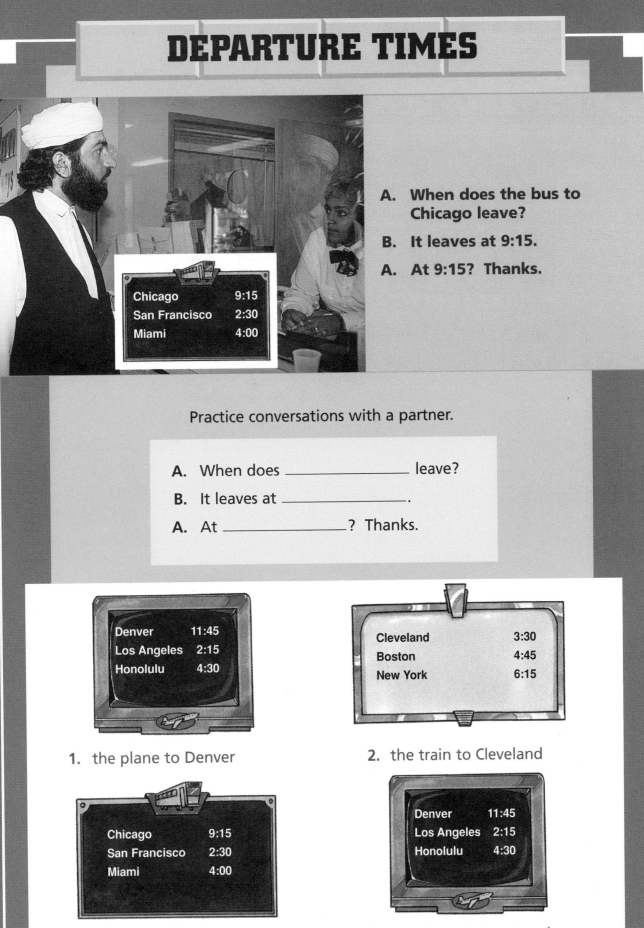

Chicago 9:15
San Francisco 2:30
Miami 4:00

A. When does the bus to Chicago leave?

B. It leaves at 9:15.

A. At 9:15? Thanks.

Practice conversations with a partner.

A. When does _____ leave?

B. It leaves at _____.

A. At _____? Thanks.

Denver 11:45
Los Angeles 2:15
Honolulu 4:30

1. the plane to Denver

Cleveland 3:30
Boston 4:45
New York 6:15

2. the train to Cleveland

Chicago 9:15
San Francisco 2:30
Miami 4:00

3. the bus to Miami

Denver 11:45
Los Angeles 2:15
Honolulu 4:30

4. the plane to Los Angeles

187

Matching

Dallas	2:30
Denver	3:00
Boston	3:15
New York	4:45
Detroit	5:30

San Diego	11:00
Santa Barbara	11:30
Los Angeles	12:15
Las Vegas	1:30
Sacramento	1:45

1. Boston   1:30
2. New York   11:00
3. .Las Vegas   3:15
4. Los Angeles   4:45
5. San Diego   12:15

6. Santa Barbara   3:00
7. Dallas   11:30
8. Sacramento   5:30
9. Denver   1:45
10. Detroit   2:30

Listening

Listen and circle the correct answer.

1. (plane)   train
2. Los Angeles   Las Vegas
3. 7:30   11:30
4. bus   1:00
5. 8:00   plane
6. 2:15   2:45

Language Experience Journal

Getting Places

How do you usually get places? Do you walk? Do you drive? Do you take the train or bus? Write about it in your Language Experience Journal. Or, tell it so your teacher can write about it. Then read your story to a classmate.

DIFFERENT CULTURES   DIFFERENT WAYS

There are many types of transportation in different places around the world.

Tell about transportation in your country.
How do people get places?
Is there a lot of traffic?
Do buses, trains, and planes leave and arrive on time?

PUT IT TOGETHER   PART Ⓐ

INFORMATION GAP ACTIVITY

Work with a partner. You each have different information about the same bus schedule. Ask each other questions to complete the schedule.

When does the bus to Boston leave?

It leaves at 1:30.

Boston	1:30
New York	4:45
Houston	2:30
Chicago	___
San Francisco	1:15
Montreal	___
Atlanta	12:00

Work with a partner. You each have different information about the same bus schedule. Ask each other questions to complete the schedule.

Boston	1:30
New York	_____
Houston	_____
Chicago	6:00
San Francisco	_____
Montreal	4:45
Atlanta	_____

When does the bus to Boston leave?

It leaves at 1:30.

Vocabulary Foundations

walk
drive
on the right
on the left
next to
across from
take
get off at
go over
bus
train
plane
turn left
turn right
uptown
downtown
interstate
expressway
exit
bridge

arrive
leave

Language Skill Foundations

I can . . .

☐ ask and give directions for getting places by foot

☐ ask and give directions for getting places by car

☐ ask for and give information about public transportation

☐ check my understanding

☐ ask about departure and arrival times of buses, trains, and planes

☐ express gratitude

☐ tell how I get places

☐ compare transportation in different countries

WEATHER
RECREATION

15

What are people doing?
What's the weather?

THE WEATHER

A. **What's the weather?**

B. **It's sunny.**

Practice conversations with a partner.

A. What's the weather?

B. _____.

1. It's cloudy.

2. It's hot.

3. It's cold.

4. It's raining.

5. It's snowing.

6. It's foggy.

What's the weather today where YOU live?

Listening

Listen and put a check under the weather expression you hear.

1. _____ _____ ✓

2. _____ _____

3. _____ _____

4. _____ _____

5. _____ _____

6. _____ _____

COMMUNITY CONNECTIONS

Look in a newspaper. What's the weather today in different cities around the country?

Place	Weather
_____	_____
_____	_____
_____	_____

RECREATION ACTIVITIES

A. What do you like to do in your free time?

B. I like to play tennis.

Practice conversations with a partner.

A. What do you like to do in your free time?

B. I like to _____.

1. play basketball

2. play soccer

3. watch TV

4. listen to music

5. bake

6. jog

7. go swimming

8. go dancing

9. roller-blade

Listening

Listen and put a check under the activity you hear.

1. ✓ _____ _____   2. _____ _____

3. _____ _____   4. _____ _____

5. _____ _____   6. _____ _____

7. _____ _____   8. _____ _____

9. _____ _____   10. _____ _____

Matching

1. watch — music
2. listen to — TV

_____

3. play — soccer
4. go — swimming

5. play — dancing
6. go — basketball

_____

7. play — cookies
8. bake — tennis

Missing Letters

1. t e n n i s
2. _ a _ _ e _ b _ l _
3. r _ l l _ r-b _ _ d _
4. _ u _ i _
5. _ _ _ e

6. s _ _ _ e _
7. _ _ i _ _ i _ g
8. _ o _
9. _ a t _ _ _ _
10. d _ _ _ _ n _

Language in Motion

What do you like to do in your free time?

I like to jog.

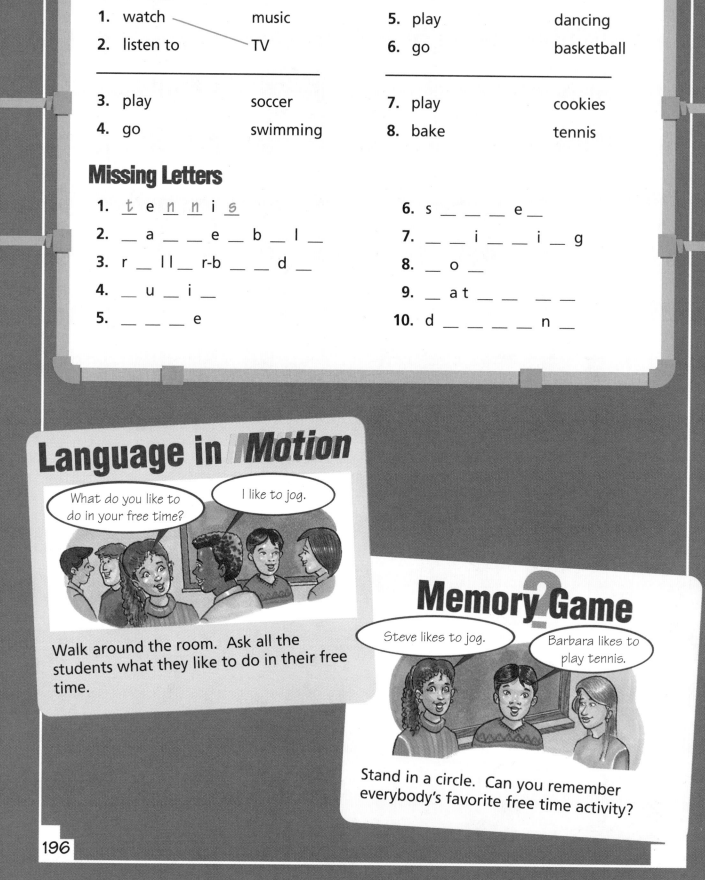

Walk around the room. Ask all the students what they like to do in their free time.

Memory Game

Steve likes to jog.

Barbara likes to play tennis.

Stand in a circle. Can you remember everybody's favorite free time activity?

PLANS FOR TOMORROW

A. What are you going to do tomorrow?

B. I'm going to see a movie. How about you?

A. I'm going to go to the park.

Practice conversations with a partner.

A. What are you going to do tomorrow?

B. I'm going to _____. How about you?

A. I'm going to _____.

1. go to a ballgame   see a play

2. play golf   play baseball

3. read   sew

4. go to a concert   relax at home

Listening

Listen and write the number under the correct picture.

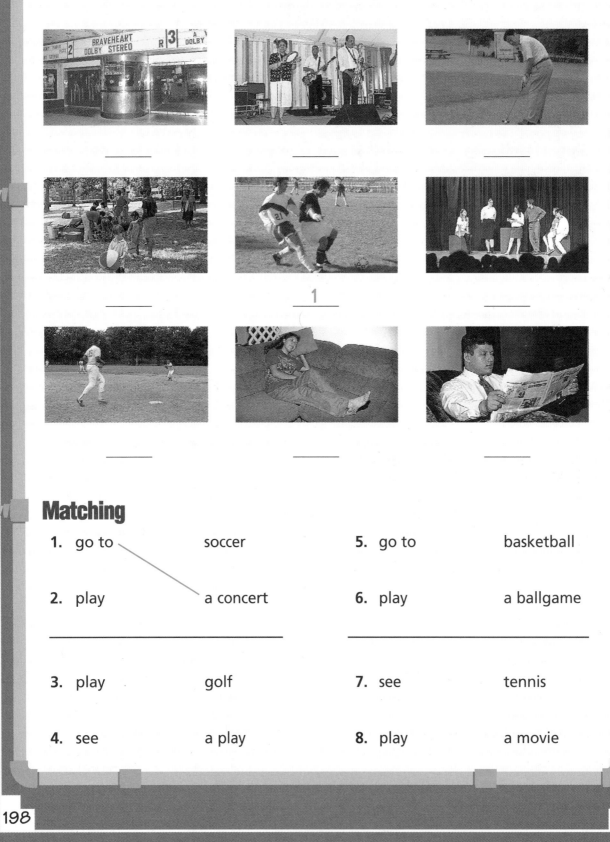

_____   _____   _____

_____   1   _____

_____   _____   _____

Matching

1. go to   soccer   **5.** go to   basketball

2. play   a concert   **6.** play   a ballgame

_____   _____

3. play   golf   **7.** see   tennis

4. see   a play   **8.** play   a movie

YESTERDAY

A. What did you do yesterday?

B. I played tennis.

Practice conversations with a partner.

A. What did you do yesterday?

B. I _____.

1. listened to music

2. watched TV

3. baked

4. went to the park

5. saw a play

6. went dancing

7. played soccer

8. went to a concert

9. relaxed at home

Construction Site

I like to **play** tennis.
I **played** tennis yesterday.

I like to **go** dancing.
I **went** dancing yesterday.

I like to **watch** TV.
I **watched** TV yesterday.

I like to **see** movies.
I **saw** a movie yesterday.

Circle the Correct Word

1. I like to ((play) played) soccer.
2. I (play   played) soccer yesterday.
3. I (watch   watched) TV yesterday.
4. I like to (watch   watched) TV after work.
5. I (go   went) to the park yesterday.
6. I like to (go   went) to the park.
7. I (play   played) golf today.
8. I like to (bake   baked).
9. I like to (go   went) dancing.
10. I (go   went) dancing yesterday.

Language Experience Journal

Last Weekend

In your Language Experience Journal, write about what you did last weekend. Or, tell your story so your teacher can write it. Then read your story to a classmate.

DIFFERENT CULTURES | DIFFERENT WAYS

People in different cultures spend their free time in different ways.

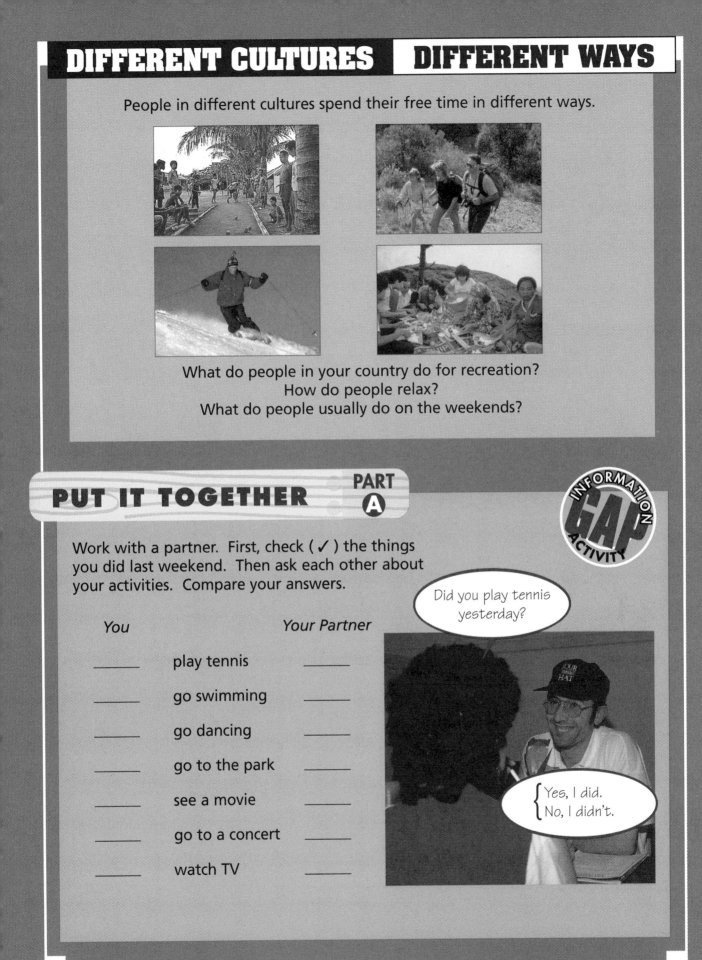

What do people in your country do for recreation?
How do people relax?
What do people usually do on the weekends?

PUT IT TOGETHER

PART A

INFORMATION GAP ACTIVITY

Work with a partner. First, check (✓) the things you did last weekend. Then ask each other about your activities. Compare your answers.

Did you play tennis yesterday?

Yes, I did.
No, I didn't.

You		Your Partner
_____	play tennis	_____
_____	go swimming	_____
_____	go dancing	_____
_____	go to the park	_____
_____	see a movie	_____
_____	go to a concert	_____
_____	watch TV	_____

Work with a partner. First, check (✓) the things you did last weekend. Then ask each other about your activities. Compare your answers.

You		Your Partner
_____	play tennis	_____
_____	go swimming	_____
_____	go dancing	_____
_____	go to the park	_____
_____	see a movie	_____
_____	go to a concert	_____
_____	watch TV	_____

Did you play tennis yesterday?

{ Yes, I did. No, I didn't. }

Vocabulary Foundations

weather
sunny
cloudy
hot
cold
raining
snowing
foggy
bake
go dancing
go swimming
go to a ballgame
go to a concert
go to the park
jog
listen to music
play baseball

play basketball
play golf
play soccer
play tennis
read
relax
roller-blade
see a movie
see a play
sew
watch TV
yesterday
tomorrow

Language Skill Foundations

I can . . .

☐ describe the weather

☐ find weather information in the newspaper

☐ name recreation activities

☐ ask about people's free time activities

☐ discuss my plans for tomorrow

☐ tell about past activities

☐ compare recreation activities in different countries

Page 4

Listen and circle.

1. A. What's your last name?
   B. Kelton.
   A. How do you spell it?
   B. K-E-L-T-O-N.

2. A. What's your last name?
   B. Brenner.
   A. How do you spell it?
   B. B-R-E-N-N-E-R.

3. A. What's your last name?
   B. Phan.
   A. How do you spell it?
   B. P-H-A-N.

4. A. What's your last name?
   B. Sanchez.
   A. How do you spell it?
   B. S-A-N-C-H-E-Z.

5. A. What's your last name?
   B. Black.
   A. How do you spell it?
   B. B-L-A-C-K.

6. A. What's your last name?
   B. Green.
   A. How do you spell it?
   B. G-R-E-E-N.

Page 7

Listen and circle.

1. A. What's your telephone number?
   B. 463-9221.
   A. Is that 463-9221?
   B. Yes. That's correct.

2. A. What's your telephone number?
   B. 948-6137.
   A. Is that 948-6137?
   B. Yes. That's correct.

3. A. What's your telephone number?
   B. 249-1115.
   A. Is that 249-1115?
   B. Yes. That's correct.

4. A. What's your telephone number?
   B. 728-0303.
   A. Is that 728-0303?
   B. Yes. That's correct.

5. A. What's your telephone number?
   B. 671-2098.
   A. Is that 671-2098?
   B. Yes. That's correct.

6. A. What's your telephone number?
   B. 837-1284.
   A. Is that 837-1284?
   B. Yes. That's correct.

Page 9

Circle the number you hear.

1. A. What's your address?
   B. 59 Central Avenue.

2. A. What's your address?
   B. 16 Blake Street.

3. A. What's your address?
   B. 30 Main Street.

4. A. What's your address?
   B. 77 Oak Street.

5. A. What's your address?
   B. 12 River Street.

6. A. What's your address?
   B. 90 Franklin Avenue.

7. A. What's your address?
   B. 44 State Street.

Page 18

Listen and put a check under the activity you hear.

1. Every day I brush my teeth.
2. Every day I read.
3. Every day I get dressed.
4. Every day I take a shower.
5. Every day I get up.
6. Every day I comb my hair.
7. Every day I go to work.
8. Every day I eat.

Page 22

Listen and put a check under the activity you hear.

1. A. What are you doing?
   B. I'm listening to music.

2. A. What are you doing?
   B. I'm watching TV.

3. A. What are you doing?
   B. I'm feeding the baby.

4. A. What are you doing?
   B. I'm studying.

5. A. What are you doing?
   B. I'm playing the guitar.

6. A. What are you doing?
   B. I'm exercising.

7. A. What are you doing?
   B. I'm washing the dishes.

8. A. What are you doing?
   B. I'm making lunch.

Page 23

Listen and circle *every day* or *right now*.

1. I study.
2. I'm eating breakfast.
3. I comb my hair.
4. I'm cleaning the house.
5. I'm relaxing.
6. I exercise.
7. I make dinner.
8. I'm making lunch.

Page 31

Listen and put a check under the classroom word you hear.

1. A. Is this your pencil?
   B. Yes. Thank you.

2. A. Where's the notebook?
   B. Over there.

3. A. Where's the desk?
   B. Over there.

4. A. Is this your eraser?
   B. Yes. Thank you.

5. A. Where's the board?
   B. Over there.

6. A. Is this your calculator?
   B. Yes. Thank you.

7. A. Where's the TV?
   B. Over there.

8. A. Is this your book?
   B. Yes. Thank you.

9. A. Where's the map?
   B. Over there.

10. A. Where's the overhead projector?
    B. Over there.

Page 36

Listen and write the number under the correct picture.

1. Open your book.
2. Raise your hand.
3. Read.
4. Close your book.
5. Go to the board.
6. Erase your name.

Page 43

Listen and put a check under the word you hear.

1. A. Tell me about the apartment.
   B. It has a very nice dining room.

2. A. Tell me about the apartment.
   B. It has a very nice bedroom.

3. A. Is there a window in the kitchen?
   B. Yes, there is.

4. A. Is there a shower in the bathroom.
   B. Yes, there is.

5. A. Tell me about the living room.
   B. It's very nice.

6. A. Tell me about the apartment.
   B. It has a very nice patio.

Page 45

Listen and put a check under the word you hear.

1. A. Where do you want this chair?
   B. Put it in the kitchen.

2. A. Where do you want this table?
   B. Put it in the dining room.

3. A. Where do you want this lamp?
   B. Put it in the living room.

4. A. Where do you want this rug?
   B. Put it in the dining room.

5. A. Where do you want this chair?
   B. Put it on the patio.

6. A. Where do you want this picture?
   B. Put it in the bedroom.

Page 53

Listen and circle the number you hear.

1. There are nine apartments in the building.
2. There are thirteen students in the class.
3. There are eight people in the room.
4. There are twenty students in the class.
5. There are sixty people in the building.
6. There are twenty-one people in the room.
7. There are ninety people in the building.
8. There are seventy people in the building.
9. There are fourteen students in the class.
10. There are sixty-nine people in the building.

Page 55

Listen and circle the time you hear.

1. A. What time is it?
   B. It's six o'clock.

2. A. What time is it?
   B. It's four o'clock.

3. A. What time is it?
   B. It's five thirty.

4. A. What time is it?
   B. It's two thirty.

5. A. What time is it?
   B. It's eleven o'clock.

6. A. What time is it?
   B. It's three thirty.

Page 57

Listen and write the time on the calendar.

1. Can you come in on Thursday at two o'clock?
2. Can you come in on Monday at three thirty?
3. Can you come in on Friday at ten forty-five?
4. Can you come in on Tuesday at eleven fifteen?
5. Can you come in on Wednesday at nine o'clock?

Page 59

Listen and circle the number you hear.

1. A. What floor do you live on?
   B. I live on the thirteenth floor.

2. A. Is this the twenty-first floor?
   B. Yes, it is.

3. A. What floor do you live on?
   B. I live on the first floor.

4. A. Is this the twenty-sixth floor?
   B. Yes, it is.

5. A. What floor do you live on?
   B. I live on the eighth floor.

6. A. What floor do you live on?
   B. I live on the twenty-seventh floor.

7. A. Is this the twelfth floor?
   B. Yes, it is.

8. A. What floor do you live on?
   B. I live on the thirtieth floor.

9. A. Is this the thirteenth floor?
   B. Yes, it is.

10. A. I live on the forty-fourth floor.
    B. The fourth floor?
    A. No. The forty-fourth floor.

Listen and put a check under the place you hear.

1. A. Where are you going?
   B. I'm going to the bus station.

2. A. Where are you going?
   B. I'm going to the drug store.

3. A. Where are you going?
   B. I'm going to the bank.

4. A. Where are you going?
   B. I'm going to the library.

5. A. Where are you going?
   B. I'm going to the department store.

6. A. Where are you going?
   B. I'm going to the laundromat.

Page 69

Listen and put a check under the place you hear.

1. A. Excuse me. Where's the hospital?
   B. Right over there.
   A. Thanks.

2. A. Excuse me. Where's the train station?
   B. Right over there.
   A. Thanks.

3. A. Excuse me. Where's the museum?
   B. Right over there.
   A. Thanks.

4. A. Excuse me. Where's the supermarket?
   B. Right over there.
   A. Thanks.

5. A. Excuse me. Where's the park?
   B. Right over there.
   A. Thanks.

6. A. Excuse me. Where's the movie theater?
   B. Right over there.
   A. Thanks.

7. A. Excuse me. Where's the restaurant?
   B. Right over there.
   A. Thanks.

8. A. Excuse me. Where's the grocery store?
   B. Right over there.
   A. Thanks.

9. A. Excuse me. Where's the library?
   B. Right over there.
   A. Thanks.

10. A. Excuse me. Where's the bank?
    B. Right over there.
    A. Thanks.

Page 70

Listen and circle the two places you hear.

1. A. Where are you going?
   B. I'm going to the bank, and then I'm going to the bakery.

2. A. Where are you going?
   B. I'm going to the park. How about you?
   A. I'm going to the museum.

3. A. Where are you going?
   B. I'm going to the post office, and then I'm going to the grocery store.

4. A. Where are you going?
   B. I'm going to the laundromat. How about you?
   A. I'm going to the shopping mall.

5. A. Where are you going?
   B. I'm going to the library, and then I'm going to the train station.

Page 82

Listen and write the number under the correct picture.

1. He's tall.
2. She's beautiful.
3. They're old.
4. We're married.
5. He's single.
6. They're young.

Page 84

Listen and write the number next to the correct picture.

1. A. What does she look like?
   B. She's short, with long gray hair.

2. A. What does he look like?
   B. He's tall, with curly black hair.

3. A. What does she look like?
   B. She's tall, with short brown hair.

4. A. What does he look like?
   B. He's short, with straight black hair.

Page 86

Listen and circle the word you hear.

1. They're old.
2. It's clean.
3. They're easy.
4. It's large.
5. It's beautiful.
6. It's very loud!

Page 90

Listen and put a check under the word you hear.

1. I'm very angry!
2. Are you thirsty?
3. I'm sick today.
4. Why are you afraid?
5. I'm very nervous today.
6. I'm very upset!

Page 95

Listen and write the number under the correct picture.

1. I'm looking for a banana.
2. There aren't any more apples.
3. There aren't any more tomatoes.
4. I'm looking for bananas.
5. I'm looking for an orange.
6. There aren't any more oranges.

Page 97

Listen and write the number under the correct picture.

1. There isn't any more milk.
2. Where's the sugar?
3. I'm looking for the bread.
4. There isn't any more cheese.
5. Where's the soup?
6. Where's the lettuce?

Listen and put a check under the foods you hear.

1. We need a bottle of soda and a dozen eggs.
2. We need a bag of sugar and a can of soup.
3. We need a loaf of bread.
4. We need a box of cookies and a pound of cheese.
5. We need a quart of milk, a bottle of soda, and a bag of sugar.

Listen and put a check under the foods you hear.

1. A. Can I help you?
   B. Yes. I'd like a cheeseburger, please.

2. A. Can I help you?
   B. Yes. I'd like a donut, please.

3. A. Can I help you?
   B. Yes. I'd like a sandwich, please.

4. A. Can I help you?
   B. Yes. I'd like coffee, please.

5. A. Can I help you?
   B. Yes. I'd like a taco, please.

6. A. Can I help you?
   B. Yes. I'd like lemonade, please.

7. A. Can I help you?
   B. Yes. I'd like a hamburger, please.

8. A. Can I help you?
   B. Yes. I'd like a pizza, please.

Listen and put a check under the item of clothing you hear.

1. I'm looking for a blue tie.
2. I'm looking for a red blouse.
3. I'm looking for a purple shirt.
4. I'm looking for a black necklace.
5. I'm looking for a brown suit.
6. I'm looking for a white shirt.

Listen and put a check under the item of clothing you hear.

1. A. May I help you?
   B. Yes. I'm looking for a pair of socks.

2. A. May I help you?
   B. Yes. I'm looking for a pair of mittens.

3. A. May I help you?
   B. Yes. I'm looking for a pair of pajamas.

4. A. May I help you?
   B. Yes. I'm looking for a pair of gloves.

5. A. May I help you?
   B. Yes. I'm looking for a jacket.

6. A. May I help you?
   B. Yes. I'm looking for a pair of shoes.

Listen and circle what you hear.

1. A. I'm looking for a belt.
   B. Belts are over there.

2. A. I'm looking for a shirt.
   B. Shirts are over there.

3. A. I'm looking for a dress.
   B. What size?
   A. Size fourteen.
   B. Size fourteen?
   A. Yes. That's right.

4. A. I'm looking for a blouse.
   B. What size?
   A. Thirty-four.
   B. Thirty four?
   A. Yes. That's right.

5. A. I'm looking for a pair of pants.
   B. What color?
   A. Gray.
   B. Gray?
   A. Yes. That's right.

6. A. I'm looking for a sweater.
   B. What color?
   A. Blue.
   B. Blue?
   A. Yes. That's right.

7. A. I'm looking for a coat.
   B. What size?
   A. Size eight.

8. A. I'm looking for a shirt.
   B. What color?
   A. Green.

Listen and write the number under the correct bills and coins.

1. I just found two dollars and twenty-five cents!
2. I just found five dollars!
3. I just found fifty dollars!
4. I just found a dollar and ten cents!
5. I just found fifty-two cents!
6. I just found thirty-five dollars!

Listen and circle the correct amount.

1. five dollars
2. ten cents
3. twenty-five dollars
4. fifty cents
5. one cent
6. seventy-five dollars
7. five cents
8. a hundred dollars

Listen and circle the amount of money you hear.

1. A. How much do I owe you?
   B. Nine dollars and ninety-five cents.
   A. Nine ninety-five?
   B. Yes. That's right.

2. A. How much do I owe you?
   B. Ten dollars and eighty-eight cents.
   A. Ten eighty-eight?
   B. Yes. That's right.

3. A. How much do I owe you?
   B. Four dollars and ninety cents.
   A. Four ninety?
   B. Yes. That's right.

4. A. How much do I owe you?
   B. Six dollars and fifty-four cents.
   A. Six fifty-four?
   B. Yes. That's right.

5. A. How much do I owe you?
   B. Fourteen dollars and fifteen cents.
   A. Fourteen fifteen?
   B. Yes. That's right.

6. A. How much do I owe you?
    B. Two dollars and twenty cents.
    A. Two twenty?
    B. Yes. That's right.

Page 127

Listen and write the number under the correct picture.

1. A. Where's the withdrawal slip?
    B. Here it is.

2. A. Where's the check?
    B. Here it is.

3. A. Where's the checkbook?
    B. Here it is.

4. A. Where's the ATM card?
    B. Here it is.

5. A. Where's the deposit slip?
    B. Here it is.

6. A. Where's the credit card?
    B. Here it is.

Page 135

Listen and write the number under the correct picture.

1. I have a backache.
2. I have a headache.
3. I have a cold.
4. I have a toothache.
5. I have a cough.

Page 137

Listen and put a check under the correct medicine.

1. I have a headache. What should I use?
2. I have a stomachache. What should I use?
3. I have a cough. What should I use?
4. I have an earache. What should I use?
5. I have a sore throat. What should I use?
6. I have a cold. What should I use?

Page 137

Listen and circle the ailment.

1. These throat lozenges will help your . . .
2. These ear drops will help your . . .
3. This cold medicine will help your . . .
4. This aspirin will help your . . .
5. These antacid tablets will help your . . .
6. This cough syrup will help your . . .

Page 140

Listen and circle.

1. A. Take one pill three times a day.
    B. I understand. One pill three times a day.
    A. That's right.

2. A. Take two teaspoons once a day.
    B. I understand. Two teaspoons once a day.
    A. That's right.

3. A. Take two capsules three times a day.
    B. I understand. Two capsules three times a day.
    A. That's right.

4. A. Take one tablet four times a day.
    B. I understand. One tablet four times a day.
    A. That's right.

5. A. Take one pill twice a day.
    B. I understand. One pill twice a day.
    A. That's right.

6. A. Take one tablet four times a day.
    B. I understand. One tablet four times a day.
    A. That's right.

7. A. Take two teaspoons after each meal.
    B. I understand. Two teaspoons after each meal.
    A. That's right.

8. A. Take one capsule before each meal.
    B. I understand. One capsule before each meal.
    A. That's right.

Page 145

Listen and write the number under the correct picture.

1. I burned my hand.
2. I twisted my ankle.
3. I cut my finger.
4. I broke my arm.
5. My arm is swollen.
6. I sprained my wrist.
7. I feel dizzy.
8. I broke my leg.
9. My neck is stiff.

Page 149

Listen and write the number under the correct picture.

1. I want to buy an aerogramme.
2. I want to mail a package.
3. I want to buy stamps.
4. I want to buy a money order.
5. I want to send a registered letter.

Page 152

Listen and write the number under the correct picture.

1. A. Excuse me. Where are the books?
    B. Over there.
    A. Thanks.

2. A. Excuse me. Where are the tapes?
    B. Over there.
    A. Thanks.

3. A. Excuse me. Where's the checkout desk?
    B. Over there.

4. A. Excuse me. Where are the magazines?
    B. Over there.

5. A. Excuse me. Where are the encyclopedias?
    B. Over there.

6. A. Excuse me. Where's the librarian?
    B. Over there.

7. A. Excuse me. Where's the card catalog?
    B. Over there.

8. A. Excuse me. Where are the dictionaries?
    B. Over there.

Page 155

Listen and put a check under the correct picture.

1. A. Who's that?
    B. That's the principal.

2. A. Who's that?
    B. That's the P.E. teacher.

3. A. Who's that?
    B. That's the guidance counselor.

4. A. Where are you going?
   B. To the nurse's office.

5. A. Where are you going?
   B. To the cafeteria.

6. A. Where are you going?
   B. To the gym.

7. A. Who's that?
   B. That's the nurse.

8. A. Where are you going?
   B. To the principal's office.

Page 157

Listen and write the number under the correct picture.

1. My favorite subject is English.
2. My favorite subject is science.
3. My favorite subject is technology.
4. My favorite subject is music.
5. My favorite subject is history.
6. My favorite subject is art.

Page 163

Listen and write the number under the correct picture.

1. A. What do you do?
   B. I'm a police officer.

2. A. What do you do?
   B. I'm a repairperson.

3. A. What do you do?
   B. I'm a delivery person.

4. A. What do you do?
   B. I'm an electrician.

5. A. What do you do?
   B. I'm a cashier.

6. A. What do you do?
   B. I'm a construction worker.

Page 165

Listen and put a check under the correct occupation.

1. I can teach.
2. I can fix sinks.
3. I can fix cars.
4. I can drive a taxi.
5. I can type.
6. I can drive a truck.

Page 168

Listen and write the number under the place where these people work.

1. I'm an assembler.
2. I'm a doctor.
3. I'm a waiter.
4. I'm a pharmacist.
5. I'm a salesperson.
6. I'm a housekeeper.

Page 170

Listen and write the number under the correct picture.

1. A. Can you use a cash register?
   B. No, I can't. But I'm sure I can learn quickly.

2. A. Can you sell clothing?
   B. No, I can't. But I'm sure I can learn quickly.

3. A. Can you repair watches?
   B. No, I can't. But I'm sure I can learn quickly.

4. A. Can you cut hair?
   B. No, I can't. But I'm sure I can learn quickly.

5. A. Can you assemble components?
   B. No, I can't. But I'm sure I can learn quickly.

6. A. Can you operate equipment?
   B. No, I can't. But I'm sure I can learn quickly.

Page 172

Listen and write the number under the correct picture.

1. A. Excuse me. Where's the employee lounge?
   B. Down the hall.
   A. Thanks.

2. A. Excuse me. Where's the Personnel Office?
   B. Down the hall.
   A. Thanks.

3. A. Excuse me. Where's the vending machine?
   B. Over there.
   A. Thanks.

4. A. Excuse me. Where's the bathroom?
   B. Over there.
   A. Thanks.

5. A. Excuse me. Where's the cafeteria?
   B. Down the hall.
   A. Thanks.

6. A. Excuse me. Where's the supply room?
   B. Down the hall.
   A. Thanks.

Page 174

Listen and write the number under the correct picture.

1. A. Careful!
   B. Excuse me?
   A. Don't go in that room!
   B. Okay. Thanks for telling me.

2. A. Careful!
   B. Excuse me?
   A. Don't smoke in here!
   B. Okay. Thanks for telling me.

3. A. Careful!
   B. Excuse me?
   A. Don't stand there!
   B. Okay. Thanks for telling me.

4. A. Careful!
   B. Excuse me?
   A. The floor is wet!
   B. Okay. Thanks for telling me.

Page 179

Look at the street scene above. Listen and circle the correct place.

1. It's on the left, across from the bakery.
2. It's on the right, next to the park.
3. It's across from the library.
4. It's on the left, next to the bank.
5. It's on the left, across from the clinic.
6. It's next to the post office.
7. It's across from the park.
8. It's on the right.

Page 182

Listen and put a check under the correct picture.

1. A. Which bus goes downtown?
    B. Bus Number 5.

2. A. Which train goes uptown?
    B. The M Train.
    A. The M Train?
    B. Yes. That's right.

3. A. Which bus goes to the mall?
    B. The Number 11 Bus.
    A. Thanks.

4. A. Which train goes to Weston?
    B. The Blue Line.
    A. The Blue Line?
    B. Yes. That's right.

5. A. Which bus goes to City Hall?
    B. Bus Number 4.
    A. Thanks.

6. A. Which train goes to the zoo?
    B. The C Train.
    A. The C Train?
    B. Yes. That's right.

Page 184

Listen and put a check next to the correct picture.

1. A. Excuse me. How do I get to the airport?
    B. Take the E Train and get off at River Road.
    A. Thanks very much.

2. A. Excuse me. How do I get to Blake's Department Store?
    B. Take Bus Number 11 and get off at Broadway.
    A. Thanks very much.

3. A. Excuse me. How do I get to City Hall?
    B. Take the Yellow Line and get off at Grand Avenue.
    A. Thanks very much.

4. A. Excuse me. How do I get to the zoo?
    B. Take Bus 9B and get off at Water Street.
    A. Thanks very much.

Page 188

Listen and circle the correct answer.

1. A. When does the plane to Dallas leave?
    B. It leaves at 9:30.
    A. At 9:30? Thanks.

2. A. When does the plane to Las Vegas leave?
    B. It leaves at 8:15.
    A. At 8:15? Thanks.

3. A. When does the bus to Toronto leave?
    B. It leaves at 11:30.
    A. At 11:30?
    B. Yes. That's right.

4. A. When does the bus to New York leave?
    B. It leaves at 9:00
    A. At 9:00? Thanks.

5. A. When does the train to Boston leave?
    B. It leaves at 8:00.
    A. At 8:00?
    B. Yes. That's right.

6. A. When does the plane to Rio leave?
    B. It leaves at 2:15.
    A. At 2:15?
    B. Yes. That's right.

Page 193

Listen and put a check under the weather expression you hear.

1. A. What's the weather?
    B. It's cold.

2. A. What's the weather?
    B. It's cloudy.

3. A. What's the weather?
    B. It's snowing.

4. A. What's the weather?
    B. It's cold.

5. A. What's the weather?
    B. It's foggy.

6. A. What's the weather?
    B. It's sunny.

Page 195

Listen and put a check under the activity you hear.

1. I like to play tennis.
2. I like to watch TV.
3. I like to go swimming.
4. I like to play soccer.
5. I like to bake.
6. I like to jog.
7. I like to play basketball.
8. I like to listen to music.
9. I like to roller-blade.
10. I like to go dancing.

Page 198

Listen and write the number under the correct picture.

1. A. What are you going to do tomorrow?
    B. I'm going to play soccer.

2. A. What are you going to do tomorrow?
    B. I'm going to see a movie.

3. A. What are you going to do tomorrow?
    B. I'm going to read.

4. A. What are you going to do tomorrow?
    B. I'm going to go to the park.

5. A. What are you going to do tomorrow?
    B. I'm going to relax at home.

6. A. What are you going to do tomorrow?
    B. I'm going to go to a concert.

7. A. What are you going to do tomorrow?
    B. I'm going to see a play.

8. A. What are you going to do tomorrow?
    B. I'm going to play golf.

9. A. What are you going to do tomorrow?
    B. I'm going to go to a ballgame.

Index of Grammar Structures

Index of Topics